Housing

Federal Policies and Programs

John C. Weicher

American Enterprise Institute for Public Policy Research
Washington, D.C.

John C. Weicher is director of the Housing Markets Program of the Urban Institute and former deputy assistant secretary for economic affairs at the U.S. Department of Housing and Urban Development.

Library of Congress Cataloging in Publication Data

Weicher, John C
   Housing.

   (AEI studies; 275)
   Includes bibliographical references.
   1. Housing policy—United States. 2. Housing subsidies—United States. 3. Home ownership—United States. I. Title. II. Series: American Enterprise Institute for Public Policy Research. AEI studies; 275.
HD7293.W36   363.5'8'0973   80–17660
ISBN 0–8447–3378–4

AEI Studies 275

Printed in the United States of America

CONTENTS

LIST OF TABLES

INTRODUCTION

The United States has had housing programs for almost fifty years. Federal activity in housing, which began in a small way under President Hoover, has gradually expanded to the point where it comprises a sometimes bewildering variety of programs. The basic housing laws of the nation fill over 1,350 pages of small print; Congress adds to this legislation at least every two years and, in addition, considers dozens of bills that it does not enact. The housing budget of the U.S. Department of Housing and Urban Development (HUD), the agency that administers many—but by no means all—of our housing programs, will be over $27 billion in fiscal year 1980, and the agency will spend over $5 billion on housing. The difference represents federal government commitments to spend money in the future; like private citizens, the government usually contracts to pay for its housing "purchases" over a long period. At present the government is obligated to spend over $230 billion to honor its past commitments, some of which continue until the year 2020.[1] About $40 billion of that amount is for housing built or subsidized under programs which are now defunct. Actual spending, however, will probably not come close to $230 billion.[2]

---

[1] The HUD budget each year provides, in technical language, "budget authority" for the government to make new commitments to subsidize housing units for a specified period of time into the future, ranging from fifteen to forty years, depending on the particular program. The amount authorized for these units in the first year of subsidy is known as contract authority. It is the pro rata share of budget authority, amounting to between 1:15 and 1:40, again depending on the program. The $230 billion represents the total budget authority still remaining from the budgets of previous years. The $5 billion in outlays is the amount of past and new budget authority that will actually be spent in the current year, including other programs in addition to subsidized housing.
[2] The budget authority requested for each unit is usually the maximum allowable subsidy for the entire period of fifteen to forty years. The maximum is calculated on the

Extensive as federal housing activity is, it constitutes a minor share of the total in our economy, a fact often forgotten in Washington. The typical American household spends about 19 percent of its income for housing,[3] a larger share than for anything else (except taxes). Two-thirds of all households own a home, and most of the remainder either have owned a home in the past or will do so. in the future. For most of them (as the truism states) the purchase of a house will be the biggest single financial transaction in their lives.

The total value of American housing is difficult to measure; it may be about $1.9 trillion (excluding land) or about 37 percent of the value of the nation's entire capital stock. A relatively small $92 billion is added to this stock annually, $65 billion in new housing and the remainder in maintenance and improvement of existing homes and apartments, but together these expenditures account for about 5 percent of the gross national product.[4] The federal government now subsidizes the housing of about 3.2 million lower-income households and has insured or guaranteed the homes purchased by another 7.9 million, which means that 64.2 million households have bought or are renting their homes without government assistance.[5]

---

assumption that the subsidized household makes no payment for its own housing. Since the programs generally require that the household pay a certain fraction of its income toward the cost of the unit, the budget in effect assumes that the household has no income—a rare occurrence. For most of the defunct programs, and in current public housing programs, the amount of the maximum annual subsidy is determined at the time a unit is constructed or first subsidized, since the amount is determined by the terms of the mortgage on the unit. Thus, as the subsidized household's income rises, the amount of subsidy declines. In addition, for most of the major defunct programs, the subsidy ends when the household's income exceeds the amount at which its required payment equals the maximum subsidy, at which point the government is no longer obligated to subsidize the household. For these programs, the budget authority substantially overstates the amount that will actually be spent. In the newer programs, however, the amount of subsidy depends on both the household's income and the rent of the unit, both of which can change over time, so that the actual amount of subsidy may be either larger or smaller than the budget assumes. A recent analysis of these programs argues that the budget authority is likely to prove too small. (See U.S. Congressional Budget Office, *The Long-Term Costs of Lower-Income Housing Assistance Programs*, 1979.) All of these programs are described in chapters 3 and 4.

[3] U.S. Bureau of the Census and U.S. Department of Housing and Urban Development, *Annual Housing Survey: 1976*, part C: *Financial Characteristics of the Housing Inventory*, Series H–150–76, 1978. The figure in the text is calculated from expense/income data in tables 2 and 3.

[4] Data on wealth are taken from U.S. Bureau of the Census, *Statistical Abstract of the United States*, 1979, p. 472; data on GNP from U.S. Department of Commerce, *Survey of Current Business*, vol. 58 (December 1978), pp. S–1, S–10.

[5] Bureau of the Census and Department of Housing and Urban Development, *Annual Housing Survey: 1977*, part A: *General Housing Characteristics*, pp. 11–13. These figures omit households which may have been subsidized in the past, or have paid off insured or guaranteed mortgages; thus the number ever assisted by the federal government is higher than the figures in the text. The difference should not be very great, however.

The present study attempts to explain federal housing policy and programs in the context of housing market conditions which result primarily from the private decisions of individuals and firms. The first chapter discusses the basic rationales that have historically been advanced on behalf of federal programs designed to promote housing consumption or production specifically. The body of the study falls into two parts, each dealing with one of these rationales for federal policy: (1) to provide decent housing for the poor (chapters 2–5); and (2) to increase homeownership among American families (chapters 6–8). Each topic begins with a review of the current housing situation and then considers federal policy. Chapter 2 discusses the quality of American housing today and how it has changed since World War II, particularly among the poor in our society. It is followed by a survey of the development of American housing policy (chapter 3), as it is the author's belief that present programs can be understood only from a historical perspective. Chapter 4 analyzes the major current housing programs—there are so many that it would be impossible to consider all of the many housing programs in any single study of reasonable length. A short chapter describing some alternatives that have recently received serious policy consideration concludes the discussion of housing subsidies. The next three chapters analyze conditions in the home purchase market, present and proposed programs designed to encourage homeownership, and special problems that may be affecting home construction costs. Chapter 9 provides a brief conclusion to the study.

It would require a much longer study than the present one to encompass all aspects of housing policy and housing production, and many areas are omitted here. In particular, no attempt is made to describe the housing finance system and the regulation of financial institutions except insofar as subsidized housing or homeownership programs are affected. Since much federal "housing" policy is really designed to affect mortgage markets rather than housing markets, this is a substantial omission. Fortunately, however, a recent, extensive review of housing finance by Patric Hendershott and Kevin Villani provides an excellent analysis and introduction to the subject.[6] Current production and operating problems of unsubsidized apartment buildings—a subject that has recently attracted substantial public attention—are also omitted from this study.

Finally, very little attention is devoted to the tax treatment of

---

[6] Patric H. Hendershott and Kevin E. Villani, *Regulation and Reform of the Housing Finance System* (Washington, D.C.: American Enterprise Institute for Public Policy Research, 1978).

housing, apart from a discussion of the effect of mortgage interest and property tax deductions on homeownership, and a brief review of the taxation of investment in rental property that focuses on the subsidized housing programs. This complex area could easily be the subject of a book in itself.[7]

---

[7] For a concise summary of present tax policy, particularly with respect to subsidized housing, see U.S. Congressional Budget Office, *Real Estate Tax Shelter Subsidies and Direct Subsidy Alternatives*, 1977.

1

The Rationales for Federal Housing Programs

Since the 1930s the federal role in housing has been justified as a means of achieving certain basic national objectives. The most important of these have been improved social conditions, especially for the poor, and a high level of economic activity. This chapter reviews the available evidence on the roles that housing in general, and federal housing programs in particular, have played in achieving these objectives.

The Social Benefits of Better Housing

When the first subsidized housing programs were enacted during the Great Depression they were advocated by many urban reformers on the basis of the theory that bad housing was the cause of—or at least a major contributing factor to—many of the social and physical problems confronting the poor. Numerous studies at the time, going back over many years, showed that a variety of social and physical ills were more common in the slums than in areas with decent housing.[1] Tearing down the slums and replacing them with good new housing was expected to reduce crime, delinquency, and antisocial behavior generally, and improve the mental and physical health of the poor. Housing was therefore provided separately from the welfare system, and in addition to it; a dollar spent on housing for the poor was expected to bring more benefits to both the poor and society than a dollar spent on food, clothing, or other commodities.

The social benefits have so far proved elusive. All available evidence indicates that crime rates are much higher than they were forty

---

[1] A review of this early literature is contained in Robert Moore Fisher, *Twenty Years of Public Housing* (New York: Harper and Brothers, 1959), chap. 3.

to fifty years ago even though housing conditions are much better; and while we have made progress against many diseases, subsequent research is finding that little of the improvement appears to be related to housing. In what is perhaps the most exhaustive recent evaluation of the research on housing and health, Stanislav Kasl of the Department of Epidemiology at Yale University reviewed 178 studies in the fields of public health, medicine, and social psychology. He concluded that

> the link between parameters of housing and indices of physical health has not been well supported by the reviewed evidence, at least not in any direct sense . . . the relationship between housing and chronic conditions and disability is not at present supported by any firm evidence . . . the association between housing and mental health (excluding housing satisfaction) is supported only by the weakest, most ambiguous studies. . . . The best designed studies do not demonstrate any mental health benefits, and it now appears that some of our most cherished hopes—such as raising educational and occupational aspirations by moving people out of slums—never will be realized.[2]

Kasl's conclusion was not entirely negative. He cited a number of studies which show that people are more satisfied when they live in better housing, which may contribute to their mental health. He noted, also, that there are certain "obvious" relationships; for example, the presence of rodents would increase the probability of rodent bites, and the lead-based paint commonly found in older buildings would contribute to the possibility of poisoning. But he found little basis for the argument that better housing leads to better health.

There is still less evidence that federal housing programs have specifically improved the health of their beneficiaries. Probably the best-known and most systematic evaluation is a longitudinal study of public housing tenants in Baltimore, conducted by Daniel Wilner and his associates at Johns Hopkins University. They compared the tenants with a similar control group living in private housing over a three-year period that spanned the move from substandard housing to the housing project. The results were mixed and did not systematically favor either group. Disease rates for persons under thirty-five, and especially for children, were significantly reduced in the project, but those for older persons were not, and there was no

---

[2] Stanislav V. Kasl, "Effects of Housing on Mental and Physical Health," in National Housing Policy Review, *Housing in the Seventies: Working Papers*, 1976, vol. 1, p. 296.

difference in death rates.[3] Even the statistically significant differences were quantitatively minor.

Studies of the relationship between housing and crime or delinquency have yielded similar results. An analysis by Bernard Lander undertaken shortly after World War II exemplifies the literature and brings out the basic methodological problem of the prewar studies used as the justification for subsidized housing programs. He found that bad housing and delinquency were strongly correlated—until education and race were taken into account, when the relationship disappeared.[4] Much of the earlier literature had ignored the possibility that the personal attributes of residents in poor housing, as well as or instead of housing conditions, might have a bearing on social problems.

Perhaps the one area in which housing quality has been linked to social problems is that of fire and fire protection. Several studies have found that fire is more common and more serious in neighborhoods with poor housing, apart from the income and other characteristics of the residents.[5] The benefit, however, that accrues from better housing is very small in relation to the cost of housing programs.

Most of the economists and others who have reviewed this literature find little evidence that better housing helps solve social and physical problems. The assessments of two leading urban economists are illustrative. Richard F. Muth of Stanford University finds that "most arguments which seek to establish a causal connection between poor housing, on the one hand, and crime and poor health, on the other, [are] tenuous at best." He adds: "There can be little doubt that crimes and health problems occur more frequently in areas of poor housing quality. This association probably arises principally because all are associated with the lower incomes of the residents of poor housing."[6] Edwin S. Mills of Princeton University is more succinct: "It is often claimed that underinvestment in slum housing breeds crime, alienation, drug abuse, and other ills. Undoubtedly, the im-

---

[3] Daniel M. Wilner et al., *The Housing Environment and Family Life* (Baltimore, Md.: Johns Hopkins University Press, 1962).

[4] Bernard Lander, *Towards an Understanding of Juvenile Delinquency* (New York: Columbia University Press, 1954).

[5] Richard F. Syron, "An Analysis of the Collapse of the Normal Market for Fire Insurance in Substandard Core Areas," Research Report No. 49 (Boston, Mass.: Federal Reserve Bank of Boston, January 1972); and John C. Weicher, "The Effect of Urban Renewal on Municipal Expenditures," *Journal of Political Economy*, vol. 80 (January/February 1972), pp. 86–101.

[6] Richard F. Muth, "The Rationale for Government Intervention in Housing," in National Housing Policy Review, *Housing in the Seventies: Working Papers*, vol. 1, p. 194.

portant causes of these problems are poverty, racial conflict, etc., none of which represent housing market failure."[7]

This conclusion is bipartisan. Muth served on President Nixon's Task Force on Urban Renewal, while Mills was a staff member of the Council of Economic Advisers under President Johnson.

These evaluations are based on scholarly research, much of it highly technical and complicated. At the same time, however, housing practitioners have been reaching similar conclusions as a result of their experiences with subsidized housing programs.[8] Federal and local housing officials, and developers of subsidized projects, have increasingly shifted from providing housing to so-called multiproblem families—especially those with children—to serving the low-income elderly. The elderly are generally regarded as the most desirable tenants because their major problem *is* their income. They may require special medical services, but they are unlikely to be problem tenants.

More than forty years' experience with public housing and other subsidized programs, and a large body of independent research findings, have provided little evidence that better housing does indeed yield benefits to society over and above the improvement in housing itself. As a result, the basic argument for subsidizing *housing* for the poor, rather than subsidizing their consumption generally by giving them money, has lost much of its force, though it is still occasionally invoked in response to proposals to fold housing programs into a general welfare reform program.[9]

Housing Production as an Economic Stimulus

The second broader purpose of federal housing activity has been macroeconomic. Since the depression, the government has sought

---

[7] Edwin S. Mills, "Housing Policy as a Means to Achieve National Growth Policy," in National Housing Policy Review, *Housing in the Seventies: Working Papers*, vol. 1, p. 209.
[8] An extreme example of the change in attitude was offered anonymously by a "close student of New York's slums" more than 20 years ago: "Once upon a time we thought that if we could only get our problem families out of those dreadful slums, then papa would stop taking dope, mama would stop chasing around, and Junior would stop carrying a knife. Well, we've got them in a nice new apartment with modern kitchens and a recreation center. And they're the same bunch of bastards they always were." (Quoted by Daniel Seligman, "The Enduring Slums," in Editors of Fortune, *The Exploding Metropolis* [Garden City, N.Y.: Doubleday and Company, 1958], p. 106.) This statement is interesting not as a characterization of public housing tenants—as such, it is grossly inaccurate—but for what it reveals about the attitude of the speaker. It exemplifies both the utopian view of many planners and reformers that bad housing was the root of many major social problems, and the actual experience that improved housing, by itself, has had little impact on behavior.
[9] Morton J. Schussheim, "Welfare Reform and Housing," speech presented before the National Association of Housing and Redevelopment Officials, Minneapolis, October 5, 1977.

to stimulate housing construction in order to increase the level of economic activity, both in the construction industry itself and in the economy as a whole. Subsidized housing production has been advocated and used as a tool of fiscal policy. Until very recently, housing construction has been countercyclical to a substantial extent because of its sensitivity to interest rates, which are high when the economy is booming and low when it is in a recession. This creates the possibility that government support for the industry may enable it to expand production relatively easily when other industries are declining and releasing resources.

This argument applies to overall housing production, not merely to subsidized housing for low-income families, and a number of programs to encourage homeownership for the "middle class" have been instituted during recessions. Unfortunately, the record of virtually all these government programs has not been impressive. For example, in 1961 the government began to subsidize interest rates on mortgages for privately owned low-income apartment projects—the Section 221 (d) (3) program—during and partly because of a recession in housing. The industry recovered without significant help from the program, however: subsidized production did not reach 10,000 starts a year until 1964, while overall production rose from 1.25 million in 1960 to 1.60 million in 1963, the third highest yearly figure recorded to that date. In a similar way the Section 8 new construction program was enacted in 1974 just before the trough of the recession in housing; however, overall production doubled, going from a rate of 1 million starts annually at the low point to more than 2 million in mid-1977, before the program had resulted in 125,000 starts.

These were new programs in both instances and therefore required administrative development before any production could begin, but the record of established programs is little better. Public housing projects have historically required about a year of federal processing before site acquisition, let alone new construction, can begin. A recent Congressional Budget Office review of federal programs concluded that public housing has had little demonstrated effect on overall housing production during its more than forty years of existence.[10]

More fundamentally, there is evidence that subsidized housing production is in large part a substitute for unsubsidized production that would probably have occurred in any case. This appears to be particularly true for the interest rate subsidy programs of the 1960s

---

[10] U.S. Congressional Budget Office, *Federal Housing Policy: Current Programs and Recurring Issues,* June 1978, p. 27.

and early 1970s, such as Section 221 (d) (3), Section 235, and Section 236. In the most recent study of substitution, Michael Murray of Duke University concludes that virtually all the starts under these programs merely replaced unsubsidized starts, because they drew mortgage funds from private lenders who would otherwise have invested in conventional mortgages.[11] Murray's results are generally consistent with an earlier analysis by Craig Swan of the University of Minnesota, who estimated that about 85 percent of the starts under Sections 235 and 236 between 1969 and 1972 would have occurred without the programs.[12] These findings are especially noteworthy because the programs are often credited with having cushioned the cyclical downturn in 1970.[13]

Murray also examined public housing and other construction financed by government and found a different pattern. About 60 percent of the subsidized units represented an increase in housing production at the time they were built. Over time, however, the rate of private construction is reduced slightly, because the public housing units cause an increase in the overall vacancy rate, thus reducing the demand for additional private housing. Ultimately, the net increase in housing production is only about one-sixth of the number of public housing units, although it takes many years for the initial increase in production to be absorbed and dissipated by market adjustment.[14]

Programs to encourage production of new homes for middle- and upper-income families may generate a greater macroeconomic stimulus. In a study of the Tandem Plan (a shallow interest rate subsidy program, described in more detail in chapters 2 and 5), Hendershott and Villani conclude that government mortgage purchases generate an increase in starts at the time they occur, but that starts in later quarters are reduced, so that there is little net stimulus over an entire business cycle.[15] This is precisely the desired effect of a countercyclical program. The conclusion is not unanimous, however; Ronald Utt finds no short-run increase in starts.[16]

---

[11] Michael P. Murray, "Subsidized and Unsubsidized Housing Starts, 1961–1977," unpublished paper, U.S. Department of Housing and Urban Development, August 1979.
[12] Craig Swan, "Housing Subsidies and Housing Starts," *American Real Estate and Urban Economics Association Journal*, vol. 1 (Fall 1973), pp. 119–40.
[13] Henry B. Schechter, "Need for National Housing Goals," paper presented at the National Association of Homebuilders, Washington, D.C., May 11, 1978, p. 3.
[14] Murray, "Subsidized and Unsubsidized Housing Starts."
[15] Patric H. Hendershott and Kevin E. Villani, "The Federally Sponsored Credit Agencies: Their Behavior and Impact," in Robert M. Buckley, John A. Tuccillo, and Kevin E. Villani, eds., *Capital Markets and the Housing Sector: Perspectives on Financial Reform* (Cambridge, Mass.: Ballinger Publishing Co., 1977), pp. 291–309.
[16] Ronald D. Utt, "An Empirical Analysis of the GNMA Tandem Plan," in Buckley et al., *Capital Markets*, pp. 363–79.

In sum, there is little evidence that federal housing policy and programs have been successful in achieving broad social and economic goals. The remainder of this book will consider how successfully they have achieved the narrower goals of improving the quality of housing and increasing the opportunities for homeownership.

2

"A Decent Home": The Quality of American Housing

The national housing goal of the United States, as established by Congress in the Housing Act of 1949, is "a decent home and a suitable living environment for every American family."[1] An explicit definition of "decent" (or, for that matter, either "suitable" or "living environment") was not and has not been formally adopted by Congress; but the reports and hearings that culminated in the 1949 act indicate the kinds of housing deficiencies that were of particular concern.[2]

In 1948 the Joint Committee on Housing addressed the problem of defining quality and, while recognizing the difficulties and the subjectivity inherent in any definition, nevertheless went on to count as substandard "the number of non-farm units . . . in need of major repairs, together with all units in urban areas which lack private inside bath and toilets."[3] This apparently represented the consensus of the time, and it has remained the basic definition of a physically substandard unit. Presidential studies of housing conditions and housing policy in both 1967 and 1973 used the same measure in estimating the number of substandard units, although coverage by then had broadened to include all rural as well as urban areas.[4]

---

[1] P. L. 87–171, Sec. 2.

[2] U.S. Congress, Joint Committee on Housing, *Study and Investigation of Housing: Hearings*, 80th Cong., 1st sess., October 1947. The following statements on housing inadequacies are typical of the opinions of witnesses from many parts of the country: P. O. Davis, director of the Extension Service of the state of Alabama, pp. 1315–16; and Power Higginbotham, mayor of Baton Rouge, p. 1670.

[3] U.S. Congress, Joint Committee on Housing, *Housing Study and Investigation: Final Majority Report* [Part 1], 80th Cong., 2nd sess., March 15, 1949, part 1, p. 9.

[4] Frank S. Kristof, *Urban Housing Needs through the 1980's: An Analysis and Projection*, Research Report No. 10, prepared for the National Commission on Urban Problems, Washington, D.C., 1968, p. 4; G.E.—TEMPO, "United States Housing Needs, 1968–1978," in *Report of the President's Committee on Urban Housing, Technical Studies*, vol. 1, 1967; National Housing Policy Review, *Housing in the Seventies*, 1974, chap. 6.

Congress was concerned about housing space as well as physical quality. In the immediate postwar period public attention centered on the number of families (especially of returning servicemen) forced to "double up" by sharing their housing with another family[5] and on those living in "overcrowded" housing—defined as a unit with more than one and a half persons per room.[6]

Trends and Current Conditions

Data on the incidence of these four measures of housing inadequacy show that there was a marked steady improvement from 1940 to 1977, to the point where very few households are living in conditions that would have been considered inadequate in 1949 (table 1). By all these measures the United States is close to achieving the goal of a decent home as it was originally conceived. (Some minimal amount of inadequate housing will probably remain, unaffected by any government policy designed to reach the national housing goal; for example, the 1977 data show some 21,000 households with incomes above $25,000 that do not have complete plumbing in their dwellings.)

The data in table 1 are aggregate figures. Similar improvements, however, have occurred in the housing of various groups of people that have frequently received special attention in housing policy. In many instances the improvements are even more pronounced for these groups than for the population as a whole, although the data have numerous gaps and changes in coverage. For example, 80 percent of nonwhite households lacked complete plumbing in 1940 compared with 7 percent of black households in 1977. The decline in overcrowding was similarly marked—from 23 percent to 3 percent. Parallel improvements occurred in rural areas, where units without plumbing dropped from 80 percent to 5 percent, and overcrowding from 14 percent to 1 percent.

Data on housing quality by income classes first became available in 1950; they show much the same pattern of progress for the poor. Of those in the poorest fifth of the population, 61 percent lived in housing without complete plumbing in 1950 compared with 7 percent in 1977. The real income of these households was rising during the period, but even for those with constant real income progress was substantial. For households with incomes of $7,500 or less in 1977

---

[5] Joint Committee on Housing, *Housing Study and Investigation,* p. 8.
[6] Ibid., part 2, "Statistics on Housing," p. 9.

13

TABLE 1

MEASURES OF HOUSING INADEQUACY, 1940–1977
(percentage of all occupied housing)

Inadequacy	1940	1950	1960	1970	1973	1977
Lacking some or all plumbing	55.4	34.0	14.7	5.5	3.6	2.4
Overall physical condition[a]	18.1	9.1	4.6	3.7	NA	2.9
Overcrowded (more than 1.5 persons per room)	9.0	6.2	3.8	2.0	1.3	0.9
"Doubling up" (married couples without own households)	6.8	5.6	2.4	1.4	1.4	1.1

NOTE: NA = Not available.

[a] "Needing major repairs" in 1940; "dilapidated" in 1950, 1960, and 1970; "poor overall structural condition" in 1977.

SOURCES: Data are from the following U.S. Bureau of the Census sources: *Sixteenth Census of the United States: 1940, Housing,* vol. 2, part 1; *1950 Census of Housing,* vol. 1, part 1; *1960 Census of Housing,* vol. 2, part 1; *1970 Census of Housing: Components of Inventory Change,* HD(4)–1; *Annual Housing Survey: 1973, United States and Regions,* part B; *Annual Housing Survey: 1977, United States and Regions,* part B; *Current Population Survey,* series P–20 (various years).

dollars (corresponding to about $3,000 in 1950), units lacking complete plumbing declined from 52 percent to 6 percent.[7]

National data on the Hispanic population only became available in the 1970 census, but the figures since then show the incidence of both overcrowding and incomplete plumbing being more than halved by 1977. This is approximately the same as the rate of improvement for blacks, rural residents, and the poorest fifth of the population and is slightly greater than the rate of improvement for households with incomes of $7,500 or less in 1977 dollars. The limitations of the data for these and other groups are often frustrating, but do not appear

---

[7] The numbers are chosen because they correspond fairly closely to the income classes used in the published reports of the various censuses. An income of $7,500 is about $1,000 above the 1977 poverty level for a family of four.

to invalidate the reported trends.[8] In each case housing remains some-what worse for the group than for the population as a whole, but the incidence of inadequacy is declining rapidly.

Physical Condition: The Problem of "Dilapidation"

The improvement in housing quality has been partly obscured by the problem of defining and measuring the overall physical condition of the unit. From 1940 through 1960, census enumerators were asked to assess the housing units that they visited. The U.S. Bureau of the Census provided a number of criteria for classifying a unit as "sound," "deteriorating," or "dilapidated" ("needing major repairs" in 1940), including pictures of homes and apartments in each cate-gory, in an attempt to minimize the degree of subjectivity in the responses.[9] Despite these efforts, a post-census evaluation in 1960 showed a high incidence of classification error, with enumerators and evaluators disagreeing over which units were dilapidated.[10] From the standpoint of attempting to estimate the total number of substandard units the error was not overly serious, since a high fraction of the misclassified units lacked complete plumbing and were thus sub-standard regardless of their overall physical condition. After exam-ining the census evaluation, Frank Kristof estimated that the classi-fication errors resulted in an understatement of substandard units by about 585,000, or 1.2 percent of the total occupied housing stock, and concluded that the issue was merely "a tempest in a teapot."[11]

Nevertheless, the Census Bureau decided to discontinue the measurement of overall housing conditions, because of its decision to conduct a mail census in 1970 as well as because of the results of its evaluation. After significant objections, particularly from city gov-

---

[8] These data are taken from the same sources as those in table 1. However, the differ-ences in coverage over time are so substantial that it is not worthwhile to attempt to construct a series of tables for the various population groups. In addition to the lim-itations mentioned in the text, there are many further problems, particularly for income classes: as 1960 data for dilapidated units are not cross-classified by plumbing facilities, the total number of units lacking complete plumbing cannot be ascertained; data on persons per room are not available for farms in 1950; data on crowding in 1960 do not identify the number of units with more than 1.5 persons per room. In addition, for reasons discussed in the next paragraph of the text, there are no data in 1970 on overall housing conditions for any of the groups; nor is there any data on doubling up for any year.

[9] U.S. Bureau of the Census, *1960 Census of Housing: Final Report*, HC(1)–1, 1963, p. 1–246. Pages 1–248 to 1–258 contain the pictures.

[10] U.S. Bureau of the Census, *Measuring the Quality of Housing*, Working Paper No. 25, 1967.

[11] Kristof, *Urban Housing Needs*, appendix C. The quotation is from page 90.

15

ernments that relied on the physical condition data, the decision was partially reversed, although the 1970 data were not collected in the way that earlier data had been. Instead, a smaller number of units were surveyed and the incidence of dilapidation was correlated with the incidence of other characteristics; then the total number of dilapidated units in the country was inferred from the overall incidence of these other characteristics.[12] The resulting numbers for 1970 are probably less reliable than the earlier data.

The Housing Goal and the 1968 Production Target

The virtual achievement of the original national housing goal is a major accomplishment of our society. At the time it was established, the goal was often ridiculed as an impossibility or an overly expensive luxury.[13] Now that it has nearly been accomplished, however, the feat attracts little attention.

One reason for this surprising attitude is that the housing goal has become confused in public discussions with two numerical production targets enunciated by Congress in 1968. The overall target was 26 million new housing units in the next ten years, 6 million of which were to be constructed for low- and moderate-income households, probably but not explicitly by means of government subsidies. These production targets are frequently referred to as the national housing goals, but in fact the legislation drew a distinction between the 1949 goal, which it reaffirmed, and the production targets, which were to be the means of substantially achieving that goal within the next decade.[14]

Once established, the production targets were soon outdated by changing political attitudes in both Congress and the executive branch of the government. Since at least 1973 these targets have had little impact on policy, and when the original ten-year period expired no new targets were set. But they have received far more attention in discussions of housing policy than the actual goal of "a decent home."

The targets were not reached; in particular, there were only about 2.7 million new or rehabilitated subsidized units, less than half of the target. (By contrast, unsubsidized production amounted to about 18½ million units, close to the 20 million target.) This shortfall has contributed to the popular perception of housing conditions. It has

---

[12] U.S. Bureau of the Census, *1970 Census of Housing*, HC(6): *Plumbing Facilities and Estimates of Dilapidated Housing*, 1973, pp. viii–xiii and appendix A.
[13] See, for example, the statement of Senator James P. Kem (R–Mo.), in *Congressional Record*, April 21, 1948, p. 4679 (Senate).
[14] P. L. 90–448, Sec. 1601(a).

16

largely been forgotten that the original target for low-income housing was based on an estimate in 1968 that there were then about 6.7 million occupied substandard units (lacking complete plumbing and/or dilapidated), and that there would be 6.3 million in 1978 in the absence of new government-subsidized production programs.[15] That 1968 estimate was essentially an educated guess, since the most recent data then available were from the 1960 census. Two years after the target was established, the 1970 census estimated that there were only about 5.3 million occupied substandard units, even though the new federal programs were barely under way; but the target was not updated. Because of the Census Bureau's decision to stop trying to count dilapidated units, we will never know how many substandard units there were in 1978; however, new data on housing quality (to be discussed in detail in the next section) suggest that there may have been around 3.8 million in 1976.

New Housing Goals

As the United States has neared the achievement of the original housing goal, the country has perhaps unconsciously sought new goals to replace it, rather than celebrating the accomplishment. This attitude is entirely reasonable, although it tends to obscure still further the extent of the actual progress; as the society becomes richer, it is possible to seek levels of well-being that formerly seemed beyond reach. Thus, new quality standards for housing have gradually been coming into use. In some cases this process has been going on for many years. The earlier standard of overcrowding (more than 1.5 persons per room) has already been superseded by a ratio of more than 1.0; this measure was used in both the 1967 and the 1973 presidential studies.[16] By this yardstick, also, the incidence of overcrowding has been declining sharply—from 15.8 percent in 1950 to 4.4 percent in 1977—and in a few years another ratio, such as 1.0 or more, may become the norm.

New standards can easily be developed for overcrowding, since the concept can be measured along a continuum. For other characteristics, unfortunately, the quality gradations are not continuous: a

---

[15] G.E.—TEMPO, "U.S. Housing Needs."
[16] Kristof, *Urban Housing Needs*, pp. 7–13; Robert Gladstone and Associates, "The Outlook for United States Housing Needs," in *Report of the President's Committee on Urban Housing, Technical Studies*, vol. 1, p. 51; National Housing Policy Review, *Housing in the Seventies*, p. 166.

house either has or lacks complete plumbing,[17] and a family either is or is not sharing its home with another family. As table 1 shows, almost no one is suffering from these problems, and indeed doubling up has virtually disappeared from public discussion of housing conditions.[18] Therefore, to measure further improvements in housing, different criteria are needed.

Fortunately, new information on housing quality is now becoming available. Partly because of the increasing obsolescence of the traditional measures of housing conditions, the U.S. Department of Housing and Urban Development (HUD) and the Census Bureau have been conducting an Annual Housing Survey (AHS) since 1973. The AHS collects data on some thirty different kinds of housing deficiencies—far more than have previously been available in any data source—for approximately a 1-in-1,000 sample of the housing stock of the United States. Questions are asked not only about the presence of facilities but also about their functioning—for example, not only, "Do you have plumbing?" but also, "Has it broken down in the last year? If so, how often? For how long?" Similar questions are asked about the heating, electrical, and other major systems of the unit.

Instead of providing a single question on overall physical condition, as in the decennial censuses, the survey covers a number of specific structural defects, such as leaky roofs, holes in floors, walls, or ceilings, or missing stairs in apartment buildings; but it also includes a new question on general housing quality, in which residents (rather than census enumerators) are asked to rate the structural condition of their dwellings. In 1977, 2.9 percent considered their housing "poor" (compared to 15.4 percent rating it "fair," 47.2 percent "good," and 34.3 percent "excellent"). Since this is the only overall quality measure now available, it has been included in the figures shown in table 1, although it may not be commensurate with the earlier census classification. About twice as many low-income households, and about three times as many blacks, rated their housing poor, but in each case the incidence of poor units was about half that of dilapidated units among the group in 1960, which suggests a substantial rate of improvement.

---

[17] Another example of gradual raising of standards can be seen in census questions about plumbing facilities. In 1940, when most units lacked complete plumbing, and in 1950, households were asked about which facilities they lacked—hot water, any running water, indoor toilet, etc. By 1970 this degree of detail was uninteresting, since nearly every unit had complete plumbing.

[18] The most recent policy discussion of this problem is in Gladstone and Associates, "Outlook for United States Housing Needs," p. 52.

TABLE 2

Selected Housing Deficiencies, 1973–1977
(percentage)

Deficiency	1973	1974	1975	1976	1977
Leaking roof	7.9	7.0	6.5	6.1	6.0
Holes in floor	2.0	1.9	1.8	1.7	1.8
Open cracks or holes in walls or ceiling	6.0	5.7	5.3	5.3	5.2
Unusable toilets[a]	3.3	3.0	2.7	2.4	2.9
Heating system breakdown	8.5	7.3	6.8	6.8	6.8

[a] Among units with only one toilet.

Source: U.S. Department of Housing and Urban Development and U.S. Bureau of the Census, *Annual Housing Survey: United States and Regions*, part B, for 1973, 1974, 1975, 1976, and 1977.

At present, data from the AHS are available for 1973 through 1977, far too short a period to establish any trends in housing quality for those attributes not previously included in the decennial census. Over its brief history, however, the AHS reports small but measurable declines in the incidence of most deficiencies. Table 2 contains data on several of the more important ones, including structural problems such as leaking roofs, holes in floors, and breakdowns in the heating and plumbing systems. The changes in the incidence of deficiencies roughly parallel the changes in the traditional measures of inadequacy reported in table 1.

Indices of Quality

The data on individual structural and system attributes have recently attracted the research interest of a number of analysts who have sought to find a new definition of standard or decent housing quality, in view of the increasing irrelevance of the original one. There have been several attempts to identify a single attribute, or a small group of attributes, that would serve as a replacement for the criterion of "dilapidation/lacking complete plumbing" that has been used for the past three decades. There is no one factor which has the obvious intuitive appeal of the old criterion, so research has centered on the relationships between the various attributes in the hope that some or many deficiencies will be found in the same units to a substantial extent—in which case one deficiency could serve as a proxy for overall housing quality. So far, this line of analysis has not been successful. Jeanne Goedert and John Goodman, for example, investigated more than twenty measures of inadequacy. They found little tendency for defects to be clustered in the same unit; instead, individual deficiencies were distributed among different units. They concluded that "no single housing feature is a reliable indicator of the presence, or absence, of a wider range of housing quality indicators . . . the prospects for developing a single, simple measure of housing quality are dim."[19]

In the absence of a simple criterion, numerous analysts have developed their own measures. Several federal agencies, including HUD, the Office of Management and Budget, and the Congressional Budget Office, have tabulated the number of inadequate units.[20] Their definitions differ in detail but generally use a similar framework and list of deficiencies. The approach can be illustrated by a recent HUD criterion that has been used in studies of the housing condition of various groups within the population. The characteristics of housing are grouped into eight categories, such as "plumbing" or "maintenance." A criterion of adequacy is then formulated for each category. These can be complex: for "maintenance" a unit is inadequate if it has at least two out of four defects (leaking roof, open cracks or holes in walls or ceiling, holes in the floor, or broken plaster or peeling paint over one square foot on walls or ceiling). Units are inadequate overall if they fail to meet the standard in any one of the eight categories.

The number of inadequate units in 1976 according to this criterion is shown in table 3, with the definitions for all eight categories. Almost 67 million occupied units had no deficiencies at all, while 7.2 million, some 9.7 percent of the total, were inadequate, down from 10.1 percent the year before. Nearly three-quarters of these were deficient in only one category. By far the most common problem was maintenance.

This definition is based on extensive analyses of housing quality by two HUD economists, Kenneth Wieand and Richard Clemmer. In addition to developing indices of housing quality, they have related

[19] Jeanne E. Goedert and John L. Goodman, Jr., *Indicators of the Quality of U.S. Housing* (Washington, D.C.: The Urban Institute, 1977). The quotation is from p. 29.
[20] U.S. Department of Housing and Urban Development, Office of Policy Development and Research, *How Well Are We Housed?: 1. Hispanics,* September 1978; Jonathan Sunshine, "Preliminary Findings of Section 8 Study," memorandum, U.S. Office of Management and Budget, October 1977; U.S. Congressional Budget Office, *Federal Housing Policy: Current Programs and Recurring Issues,* 1978, p. 6.

TABLE 3

Housing Quality in 1976

(units in thousands)

Type of Flaw[a]	Units with Flaw		Inadequate Units by Number of Flaws				
	Number	Percent	1	2	3	4	5+
Plumbing	1,946	2.6	522	656	504	238	26
Kitchen	1,342	1.8	311	356	421	228	26
Maintenance	3,046	4.1	2,243	456	137	185	26
Public hall	303	0.4	199	84	14	6	0
Heating	1,156	1.6	864	149	62	64	19
Electrical	68	0.1	19	26	13	2	8
Sewage	945	1.3	0	242	445	233	26
Toilet access	1,352	1.8	1,126	201	23	2	0

[a] Definitions: *Plumbing*: unit lacks or shares complete plumbing facilities; *Kitchen*: unit lacks or shares a complete kitchen; *Sewage*: unit lacks public sewage, septic tank, or cesspool for sewage disposal, or has no chemical toilet; *Heating*: unit has no means of heating, or is heated by unvented room heaters, fireplace, stove, or space heater (outside South Census Region); *Maintenance*: unit suffers from any two of the following four defects: leaking roof, open cracks or holes in interior walls or ceiling, holes in interior floor, or broken plaster or peeling paint over one square foot on interior walls or ceilings; *Public hall*: unit suffers from any two of the following three defects: public halls lacking light fixtures, loose or missing steps found on common stairways, stair railings missing or not firmly attached (only in multifamily buildings having common halls or stairways); *Toilet access*: access to sole flush toilet is through one or two or more bedrooms used for sleeping (applies only to households with children under eighteen years old); *Electrical*: unit has exposed wiring, fuses, or circuit breakers which have blown three or more times in the previous ninety days and lacks wall outlets in at least one room (must have all deficiencies to be considered inadequate).

Source: Adapted from U.S. Department of Housing and Urban Development, Office of Policy Development and Research, *How Well Are We Housed?: 1. Hispanics*, September 1978, tables 3 and 4.

the number of deficiencies in a unit to its rent or price and to the income of its occupants. Wieand and Clemmer find that units rated inadequate solely because of maintenance problems appear to be valued as highly as those with no deficiencies and are typically occupied by families with the same income. For units with other defects—such as incomplete plumbing or inadequate heating systems—values, rents, and incomes are all markedly lower. What is most important is that values, rents, and incomes decline steadily as the number of deficiencies increases.[21]

These findings indicate that housing quality should probably be measured by an index of deficiencies rather than by one or two specific attributes if it is to be measured at all adequately in the future. Units with more than one deficiency appear to be quite different in quality from those with only one deficiency (which appear to fit into a category that might be called high substandard).

Expense/Income Ratios

In recent years an alternative method of measuring housing inadequacy has been employed by several analysts. Instead of attempting to define physical quality they concentrate on the financial aspect, looking at the cost of housing as it compares to the income of the residents. Typically, the cost measure used is a rent/income ratio: drawing on the common rules of thumb among mortgage lenders and family financial planners, a ratio greater than 0.25 is taken as evidence of financial hardship, and therefore of a housing problem.[22] Such a ratio is frequently used by mortgage lenders in evaluating loan applications: if the mortgage payment, property taxes, and mortgage insurance (if any) exceed 25 percent of the applicant's income the application is likely to be rejected. A similar ratio is often used by family financial advisers for renters. Rent/income ratios, of course, by definition refer only to renter households, but until the AHS there were virtually no data on housing expenses for owner/occupants, and thus no corresponding expense/income ratios could be constructed.

Unlike the various measures of physical deficiencies, the overall rent/income ratio and the fraction of renters paying more than 25 percent of their income for rent have been rising steadily over time, from 31 percent in 1950 to 32 percent in 1960, 39 percent in 1970, 38 percent in 1973 (a slight decline), and 46 percent in 1977. Data for owners are available since 1974, and show an increase also, but the

---

[21] Kenneth F. Wieand and Richard Clemmer, "The Annual Housing Survey and Models of Housing Services Output," paper presented at the Conference of the American Real Estate and Urban Economics Association, May 1977; Kenneth F. Wieand, "Analysis of Multiple-Defect Indicators of Housing Quality with Data from the 1976 Annual Housing Survey," unpublished paper prepared for U.S. Department of Housing and Urban Development, Office of Policy Development and Research, Office of Economic Affairs, 1978.

[22] For example, David Birch et al., *America's Housing Needs: 1970 to 1980* (Cambridge, Mass.: Joint Center for Urban Studies, 1973), pp. 4–4 to 4–6. This report uses a rent/income ratio of 0.35 or more for elderly or single-person households to measure "high rent burden," and 0.25 for all other households.

level is much lower; the fraction had risen from 19 percent to 23 percent by 1977.[23] Taken all together, some 31 percent of all households (or 20.0 million) are paying more than 25 percent of their income for housing, far more than the 4.8 million living in units without complete plumbing or with more than one person per room, or the 7.2 million living in inadequate housing according to the HUD definition.

The rent/income ratio is simpler, and thus may have more intuitive appeal, than any index of housing deficiencies, and its use is increasing in policy discussions, but it is a fundamentally inadequate measure of housing quality. Expenditures on housing are determined simultaneously by supply and demand in housing markets: they may change when either changes. The rising rent/income ratio is usually regarded as evidence of a decrease in supply or a rise in price, and therefore as evidence of a "problem," without reference to the demand side of the market. Rising prices may well affect housing expenditures, of course, but so also may rising incomes or changing tastes among the population.

All of these factors have been changing over the postwar period. Rents have been rising less rapidly than have other prices, while the relative cost of buying and operating a home has gone up. Incomes have increased substantially. Only if both the price and income elasticities of demand were unity would expenditures for housing be expected to remain stable over time in relation to income. Research on these elasticities suggests that both may be fairly close to unity or slightly above it.[24] These research findings imply that rent/income ratios should be rising (and in fact they have done so), while expense/income ratios for homeowners could be either rising or falling, depending on whether the increase in price affects behavior more strongly than the increase in income. The declining relative price of rental housing also implies that renters could in fact lower their rent/income ratios and remain in the same quality of housing that they have been occupying. Instead, most renters have apparently chosen to live in better housing.

Over the same period tastes have been changing also, as the age distribution and family structure of the population have changed. In particular, a rising proportion of the elderly have chosen to live apart from their children and families when they retire. The elderly typically have higher expense/income ratios for housing than those of the rest

---

[23] These data are taken from the same sources as the information in table 1.

[24] Frank de Leeuw, "The Demand for Housing: A Review of Cross-Section Evidence," *Review of Economics and Statistics*, vol. 53 (February 1971), pp. 1–10.

of the population, in part because they are able to finance their current expenditures on housing out of past savings.

Another factor affecting rent/income ratios is the growth of "in-kind" welfare programs in recent years, under which low-income households receive goods, such as food stamps or medical services, rather than money income. These in-kind transfers enable low-income households to spend larger fractions of their cash income on the goods that are not subsidized, including housing (for all those not living in subsidized housing); as a result, they can afford to incur high rent/income ratios.

While the expense/income ratio is thus a misleading indicator of housing adequacy, the growth in its popularity is nevertheless indicative of an important change in American housing: we have passed a significant milestone in housing quality, reaching the point where physical inadequacy is so infrequent that we can no longer usefully analyze housing quality by means of simple physical measures.

The Causes of Housing Improvement

Most of the foregoing discussion has looked backward—to the establishment of the national housing goal in 1949 and to what has happened since. But public policy typically looks forward. From a policy maker's standpoint it is not appropriate merely to take note of the achievements of the past thirty years. New goals have become feasible, replacing the older ones; these new goals will, of necessity, be reached in the future. But the record of the past and the conditions of the present are relevant to the selection of both goals for the future and means to reach those goals. In particular, it is helpful to know not only how far we have come but how we got there—in other words, to know what policies or phenomena have been responsible for the improvement in housing quality.

There are many possible explanations for this improvement, but housing analysts have concentrated on three factors, finding indications that each has had some impact:

1. Federal programs, such as public housing, designed to eliminate substandard housing and replace it with better units
2. Rising incomes for the population, including the poor
3. A decline in the price of housing in comparison with that of other goods

Of these phenomena, the first is the result of explicit government activity and the second is primarily the result of activity in the private sector. The third is potentially the result of both: prices may fall because of technological improvements in housing construction or because of government programs that increase the supply of housing.

There is some prima facie evidence for each hypothesis. Since 1950 the federal government has subsidized the construction of over 2.4 million apartments and 500,000 homes for lower-income families and has also subsidized over 50,000 existing apartments and 800,000 existing homes. The latter do not increase the total stock of housing, but the subsidies can generate quality improvements. At the same time, however, at least 13.1 million units lacking complete plumbing were either removed from the stock or upgraded over the same period, and 3.3 million fewer units were crowded by 1977, so the programs clearly cannot be given full credit for the improvement.

Also, since 1950, real income per family has risen by about 85 percent, a growth rate of about 2.4 percent per year; income for the poorest 20 percent of the population has risen at almost exactly the same rate. As has been mentioned in the discussion of rent/income ratios, the rents on apartments have risen less rapidly than other items in the cost of living, but the cost of homeownership has risen more rapidly. From 1953 to 1977 the rent component of the consumer price index (CPI) has increased by 91 percent while the cost of homeownership has risen by 173 percent; the overall CPI has risen by 127 percent. The annual rates of increase are 2.7, 4.3, and 3.5 percent, respectively. (The year 1953 is chosen as the base for these comparisons because it was the first year for which the cost of homeownership was computed. Before 1953 the overall CPI had also increased at a more rapid rate than its rent component.) Since 1977, of course, the CPI and all of its components have increased at a faster rate, but the relative growth of the rent and homeownership indices shows the same pattern.

There have been a few more sophisticated analyses of the improvements in housing quality. Research has been hampered by the paucity of annual data on housing: too many factors are changing simultaneously over a decade to permit any reliable disentangling of their separate contributions to housing improvement. To avoid this problem, some analysts have attacked the question indirectly by comparing the changes between metropolitan areas, cities, or neighborhoods from one census to the next and relating the changes in quality to the changes in housing construction, in incomes, or in prices. In the most recent study, Weicher, Yap, and Jones analyze changes in substandard housing from 1960 to 1970 in the 50 largest metropolitan areas, and also examine the level of substandard housing as of the mid-1970s for 60 large SMSAs. In both cases, they find less low-quality housing in areas where there is a high rate of private new housing construction, relative to household formation, even though the private new units are occupied by relatively high-income households who certainly did not live in substandard housing before moving in. Private production has the greatest impact on substandard housing; other somewhat less important variables include income and demographic factors, particularly the incidence of racial and ethnic minorities. An increase in income reduces the incidence of deficient units, as would be expected. A high percentage of and growth in minority households are associated with a high level of substandard housing, reflecting either discrimination or the lower levels of wealth accumulated by minority households, or both.[25]

This result is consistent with the popular notion that a "filtering" process occurs in housing markets. In this process, prices for lower quality housing fall when higher quality units are built, because consumers have a wider choice of housing. When the new units are built, the households moving into them vacate high-quality housing, which families of somewhat lower income then occupy, leaving their former housing vacant in turn. A sequence of moves continues until ultimately, at the bottom of the quality distribution, low-income families move from substandard to standard housing, and the substandard units drop out of the stock. This filtering hypothesis has been both advocated and attacked by academic analysts of housing markets for at least three decades. It is controversial because it implies that government housing assistance for higher priced homes, insofar as it increases the supply of housing, will lead to a gradual movement into better housing throughout the distribution of housing quality, and thus provides a rationalization for subsidies to relatively well-to-do families.[26]

Of particular interest for housing policy is a finding that government production of subsidized housing for low- and moderate-income households directly has only a short-run effect on the incidence of substandard housing. In the first five years after it is built, the subsidized unit appears to generate an improvement in housing quality, but after ten years, the effect disappears. The pattern occurs for each major housing program, including public housing, Section 235,

---

[25] John C. Weicher, Lorene Yap, and Mary S. Jones, *National Housing Needs and Quality Changes during the 1980s* (Washington, D.C.: The Urban Institute, 1980), chap. 9.

[26] For a review of this literature, see John C. Weicher, " 'A Decent Home': An Assessment of Progress toward the National Housing Goal and Policies Adopted to Achieve It," in Donald Phares, ed., *A Decent Home and Environment: Housing Urban America* (Cambridge, Mass.: Ballinger Publishing Company, 1977), pp. 148–51. The most rigorous theoretical analysis of filtering is James L. Sweeney, "A Commodity Hierarchy Model of the Rental Housing Market," *Journal of Urban Economics*, vol. 1 (July 1974), pp. 288–323.

and Section 236; none seems to bring about any long-term improvement in housing conditions.[27]

Other studies tend to show that income is the most important
factor affecting the incidence of substandard housing, but they either
omit private and subsidized housing production from the analysis or
suffer from major data problems. Davis, Eastman, and Hua, for example, analyzed the change in housing units without complete
plumbing from 1960 to 1970 among the central cities of the fifty largest
SMSAs, finding that it was correlated with the change in the incidence
of poverty. They also attempted to study changes in substandard
housing over this period, but lacked data on physically dilapidated
units; the limited information collected in the 1970 census was not
published until after their study was completed.[28] Previously, Richard
Muth analyzed differences between cities in 1950 and concluded that
income increases were primarily responsible for the decline in substandard housing during the 1950s. He did not study the effect of
government programs.[29]

While these results are not conclusive, they tend generally to
show that private housing production and income increases are the
major contributing factors to housing quality improvement. They
provide little justification for the argument that government programs
have been primarily responsible.

Who Lives in Substandard Housing?

Perhaps as important for future policy as the reasons for past improvements is information on who at present lives in inadequate
housing. Housing programs can be—and frequently are—targeted
for specific groups within the population, on the basis of income,
age, location, or other factors. Even when a program is not explicitly
directed to a particular group it is helpful to know the characteristics
of the households most likely to be served by it.

The dominant attribute of the small number of households still
living in housing that is not decent, according to the standards of
1949, is the fact that they are poor.[30] Poor people are found more

---

[27] Weicher, Yap, and Jones, *National Housing Needs*, chap. 9.

[28] Otto A. Davis, Charles M. Eastman, and Chan-I Hua, "The Shrinkage in the Stock
of Low-Quality Housing in the Central City: An Empirical Study of the U.S. Experience
over the Last Ten Years," *Urban Studies*, vol. 11 (February 1974), pp. 13–26.

[29] Richard F. Muth, *Cities and Housing* (Chicago, Ill.: University of Chicago Press, 1969),
chap. 10.

[30] These statements are based on multiple regression analyses of the deficiencies, made
through use of the 1974 AHS computer tapes. This is also the source for the results
summarized in table 4.

frequently in the units lacking complete plumbing, and they are disproportionately crowded (by either the 1.0 or 1.5 criterion). No other characteristic defines these households as sharply. To a lesser extent, married couples occupy better housing than do other household types for a given income level. Single persons and families headed by an unmarried man or woman more frequently live in housing without complete plumbing, but on the other hand they suffer from overcrowding less frequently. The same is true of the elderly, while young households (with the head less than thirty-five years old) seldom experience either deficiency.

Perhaps surprisingly, race appears to be a minor factor. Blacks show a pattern similar to that of the elderly and the nonmarried household types. Hispanic-Americans, however, present a very different pattern: they live in homes with complete plumbing as frequently as non-Hispanic whites or other races, and are crowded less frequently than any other racial or ethnic group.

Housing quality also differs by location. Historically, the worst housing has been found in the South and in rural areas, and this continues up to the present, although crowding is rarely found on farms.

With the advent of the Annual Housing Survey, information has become available on a greater number of deficiencies. Table 4 presents a summary of a statistical analysis of the frequency with which households of various types live in housing suffering from any of twenty-six separate defects, including incomplete plumbing and overcrowding as well as the newer measures. Income is, again, the most important distinguishing characteristic: nearly all of the deficiencies are found more frequently in the housing of the poor. (The two found *less* frequently are presence of a subfamily and leaky basements; the former is to be expected, as the income of the subfamily is counted with the income of the main family for the purpose of measuring the total household income.)

Family composition is next in importance. Households headed by a female (defined as those with no male adult present) suffer disproportionately from about three-quarters of the defects, and other unmarried households from more than half; households in the South and in rural areas also experience more than half. On the other hand, race and age appear to have relatively little impact. Young families suffer from slightly less than half the defects but live in better housing than their elders for about one-quarter of the measures. The elderly and Hispanic-Americans generally live in *better* housing than do other households; blacks and other races are hardly distinguishable from whites.

To avoid confusion it should be stressed that in these compu-

TABLE 4

INCIDENCE OF TWENTY-SIX DEFICIENCIES, BY HOUSEHOLD TYPE, 1974

Household Type	Higher Incidence Than Normal	Lower Incidence Than Normal
Poor	23	2
Black	3	1
Hispanic	4	12
Other race	4	0
Young (under 35)	11	6
Old (over 65)	1	8
Household with children	13	4
Male head, no wife	14	0
Female head	19	3
Single person	15	4
Living in South	16	2
Living in central city	2	11
Living in rural area	16	2

NOTE: For a list of the twenty-six deficiencies, see the appendix.

SOURCE: U.S. Department of Housing and Urban Development, Office of Policy Development and Research, Annual Housing Survey, tabulations from computer tape files.

tations the economic assumption of ceteris paribus is employed: the table refers to households which are identical in all particulars except the one in question. Thus, the information on blacks refers to the difference between blacks and whites holding constant their income, family composition, age, and location. Typically, blacks live in worse housing than whites, but the analysis summarized in table 4 indicates that this occurs primarily because they are poorer, live less frequently in husband/wife households, and are more heavily concentrated in the South. In the same way, the table shows that people living in the South usually live in worse housing than elsewhere, even after differences in income, race, family structure, age, and urban/rural location are taken into account.

The results in table 4 are similar to those reported by Goedert and Goodman, who also examined twenty-six measures of inadequacy and found all of them disproportionately concentrated among the poor. They, too, found inadequacy to be more frequent in rural areas, even taking income into account.[31]

These findings can most appropriately be regarded as prelimi-

---

[31] Goedert and Goodman, *Indicators of Quality*, pp. 15–20.

nary; there is room for a substantial volume of additional work on the quality of the housing occupied by specific groups within the population. But the results so far are strong and consistent: people living in inadequate housing are poor, first and foremost. To a lesser degree they live in rural areas and the South, and they do not live in the traditional husband/wife family. Until further information becomes available, housing policy should be based on an understanding of these facts.

3

The Historical Development
of Subsidy Programs

This chapter briefly reviews the history of housing subsidies for lower-income families in order to provide a background for understanding the current programs, which are discussed in chapter 4. The development of housing subsidies has been a process of evolution in which programs have been modified gradually in the light of experience and new programs have grown out of old ones. Many ostensibly new programs are in fact resurrections of earlier ones or are combinations of elements from several previous programs.

The First Subsidies

Federal housing programs had their beginnings during the Great Depression, under President Hoover.[1] In 1932 the Reconstruction Finance Corporation (RFC) was empowered to make loans to private limited-dividend corporations whose sole purpose was providing housing for low-income families. Both rents and rates of return were to be regulated by states or cities. New York was the only state in which such corporations were in existence, and only one project was financed by the RFC although several other states passed enabling statutes.

President Roosevelt transferred this activity to the newly created Public Works Administration (PWA), which was authorized by the National Industrial Recovery Act to construct or finance public works,

---

[1] A review of federal housing subsidy programs prior to the U.S. Housing Act is contained in Gilbert A. Cam, "United States Government Activity in Low-Cost Housing, 1932–38," *Journal of Political Economy*, vol. 47 (June 1939), pp. 357–78. The legislative history of the subsidy programs is summarized in Milton P. Semer et al., "A Review of Federal Subsidized Housing Programs," in National Housing Policy Review, *Housing in the Seventies: Working Papers*, 1976, vol. 1, pp. 82–144.

including low-cost housing and slum clearance. The federal government continued to offer long-term mortgage loans to limited dividend companies to build and operate the units. This program was terminated early in 1934, however, because the rents were expected to be much higher than low-income families could afford.

The federal government then began building the units directly rather than financing private firms to do so. The Housing Division of PWA began to buy land, design housing, and advertise for construction bids in various cities. To a substantial extent this land was located in slum areas.

The federal government sought to buy the land from the individual owners, instituting blanket condemnation proceedings against those unwilling to sell. When an owner in Louisville sued the government, arguing that such condemnation was unconstitutional, the federal district court ruled in his favor in 1935 and the court of appeals upheld the decision.[2] The government suspended the program pending an appeal to the Supreme Court and then in 1936 decided not to appeal, terminating the program.

Abortive as this initial effort proved to be, it nevertheless prefigured later programs in several important ways. The basic purpose of the program was to promote economic recovery by creating employment, not to improve the housing of low-income families. The focus on production rather than consumption was strikingly exemplified when President Roosevelt in 1935 rescinded over half the funds for the program, on the basis that alternative public works provided more jobs in a shorter time. Relatively little housing (about 3,100 units in seven limited dividend projects) was built under this legislation. An additional seventeen projects were completed by the PWA by mid-1937, and thirty-four were under construction. Total housing units in all fifty-one projects amounted to about 21,600 units. This was not a very effective means of stimulating the economy, as President Roosevelt recognized.

The mechanics of the program drew a distinction between construction and finance that has been common to most subsequent programs. The federal government did not originally intend to build and operate the housing but, rather, to make loans to private firms to do so. The government undertook construction and management activity only when private firms appeared to be too slow to bring about the desired economic stimulus.

The limitation on dividends has been part of several later pro-

---

[2] United States v. Certain Land in the City of Louisville, Jefferson County, Kentucky, 9 Fed. Supp. 137 (Jan. 4, 1935), 78 Fed. 2d 684 (July 15, 1935).

grams providing subsidies for privately owned housing. It apparently reflects the view that profits are an important component of housing costs, and that if profits are limited rents on new apartments can be lowered substantially, and poor families will be able to afford them. As has been mentioned, this did not prove to be the case in 1934.

Public Housing

The years from 1935 to 1937 were spent in formulating and passing the legislation that established the public housing program. Bills were introduced in both houses of Congress in 1935 and became the occasion of an extended debate over the purposes of federal housing subsidies. Builders and labor unions advocated housing construction as a means of providing employment and stimulating the economy, while public health officials and urban reformers were concerned with the health and social benefits to be derived from slum clearance. Some housing analysts argued that subsidies were necessary to enable low-income families to live in new housing because private enterprise would not build homes for the poor. Opposition to subsidized construction was voiced by the U.S. Chamber of Commerce and the savings and loan associations, which advocated a program of rent subsidies to individual families, who would use them to pay the cost of living in housing of their own choice—presumably privately owned existing apartments.

The proponents of subsidized construction prevailed with the Congress. After a public housing bill failed in 1936, passing the Senate but dying in the House, Congress in 1937 approved the U.S. Housing Act.[3] This legislation provided for federal payments for the construction of new apartments for low-income families. A construction cost limit of $5,000 per unit was established. The occupants would be required to meet operating expenses and utilities from their own incomes. The Louisville court decision mentioned above was effectively circumvented by a provision that the federal subsidies would be paid to state and local housing agencies, which could themselves exercise eminent domain. The first such agency had been established in Ohio in 1933. These local authorities would also operate the projects after they were built.

The precise mechanism for the federal subsidy was somewhat complicated. The local authority sold its own bonds to private individuals and institutions; these bonds were tax exempt and also carried a federal guarantee of the timely payment of principal and interest.

---

[3] U.S. Housing Act of 1937, P. L. 75–412.

The federal government then paid the local authority, which in turn paid the bondholder.

In the forty years since the creation of this program about 1.1 million units have been built.[4] Under the original 1937 act some 160,000 were built over a period of twelve years, most of them during World War II to provide housing for war workers, in many cases regardless of their incomes. The 1949 Housing Act[5] expanded the program substantially, and another 155,000 units were begun in the next three years. Production was then cut back sharply, but not quite to its pre-1949 levels: the number of units started ranged from 15,000 to 35,000 per year until the late 1960s. A surge in production from 1968 to 1971, with over 300,000 units begun, was followed by another sharp cutback. The program was suspended in 1973 and was reactivated in 1976.

In part these changes in policy have coincided with changes in political administration (in 1952, for example), but this has not always been the case. The expanded program that began in 1968 under President Johnson continued for three years under President Nixon. Conversely, the transition from President Eisenhower to President Kennedy was not marked by any notable increase in public housing. In the last two decades, at least, the political vagaries of the program seem to have been caused more by general public perceptions of its successes and failures than by changes of party in power.

Rents and Income Limits. The 1937 act limited the income of public housing tenants to five times the rent they would have to pay (that is, the operating costs of the unit, since capital costs were paid by the federal government). This limit remained in force until 1959, although there were exceptions for large families (an income of six times the rent), and after 1949 various exemptions from income were permitted, which effectively raised the original limit.

A lower bound on income was implicit in the form of the subsidy. Those families that could not afford to pay the operating costs were excluded, even though the act defined the eligible population as "families who are in the lowest income group." This was clearly understood by Senator Robert Wagner (D–N.Y.), the chief sponsor: "Obviously this bill cannot provide housing for those who cannot pay the rent minus the subsidy allowed," he observed to Senator Claude Pepper (D–Fla.).[6]

---

[4] Unless otherwise indicated, data on housing programs are taken from U.S. Department of Housing and Urban Development, *1978 HUD Statistical Yearbook*, 1980.
[5] Housing Act of 1949, P. L. 81–338.
[6] Quoted in Semer et al., "Review of Housing Programs," p. 102.

In 1959 Congress changed the law to give the local housing authorities the right to set income limits and rents.[7] During the 1960s most authorities set the rents for most individual tenants in proportion to their incomes, but high enough to cover operating costs. Gradually, however, rent/income ratios crept upward, as operating costs began to rise much more rapidly than tenant incomes, primarily as a result of the general inflation suffered by the economy after about 1965.[8]

Congress reacted to this situation by expanding the federal payment to include part of the operating costs as well as all of the capital costs. This was designed to bring public housing within the economic reach of those who were so poor that they could not afford to pay even the operating costs of their apartments without spending "too much" of their income on housing. Congress also limited the rent of a public housing tenant to 25 percent of his or her income if this was less than operating costs; this substantially changed the nature of the subsidy from one conditioned on part of the cost of the unit to one conditioned on income. This legislation is known as the Brooke Amendment, after its chief sponsor, Senator Edward Brooke (R–Mass.).[9]

The legislative change coincided with court decisions limiting the ability of local housing authorities to select their tenants from among the eligible applicants. As a result, tenant incomes have declined in real terms over the past decade. For each year during the 1950s and 1960s, the typical family admitted to public housing had an income of about $2,500 in 1967 dollars.[10] By 1978 this had declined to about $2,000. Tenants were poorer in relative terms as well. The typical 1967 family was in about the tenth percentile of the income distribution (meaning that 90 percent of American families had higher incomes), while the 1978 family was in the fifth percentile. At the same time the fraction of tenants that were employed was apparently declining. Slightly more than half of the households in 1967 were receiving public assistance or benefits such as social security, so that

---

[7] Housing Act of 1959, P. L. 86–372.

[8] Frank de Leeuw, *Operating Costs in Public Housing: A Financial Crisis* (Washington, D.C.: The Urban Institute, 1974), chap. 3.

[9] Housing and Urban Development Act of 1969, P. L. 91–152, Sec. 213(a).

[10] U.S. Department of Housing and Urban Development, Housing Assistance Administration, *Families Moving into Low-Rent Housing, Calendar Year 1966,* January 1968, pp. 4–5. Data on the characteristics of public housing tenants are not collected for all tenants annually: information is available for newly admitted tenants and for those recertified for occupancy. The cycle for recertification is about three years. Data on recertified tenants show a similar income change: U.S. Department of Housing and Urban Development, Housing Assistance Administration, *Families in Low-Rent Projects: Families Reexamined during Calendar Year 1966 for Continued Occupancy,* April 1968, pp. 6–7, 18–19.

nearly half, if not more, would have had a worker in the family;[11] in 1978 only 30 percent of the households reported that someone was working.

The Brooke Amendment and subsequent legislation have had a substantial impact on the cost of the program as well. By 1977 operating subsidies amounted to about 35 percent of total federal expenditures, or over half as much as interest on the bonds, and about 35 percent of total operating income for the local authorities.

Turnkey Programs. Under the original public housing program the projects were designed by the local housing authority and built by private contractors to the authority's specifications. This was modified during the 1960s, however, to permit purchase of new, privately designed and built projects (the Turnkey programs). Almost 250,000 such units were acquired by local authorities. In 1965, public housing was extended to the existing housing stock under the Section 23 leased housing program.[12] Local authorities could sign leases with private landlords, and the federal government would make the same subsidy payments that it made for new units. The program was not large—it encompassed about 65,000 units by 1972—but it was a departure from previous policy with significant implications for the future.

Urban Renewal

During the 1940s the public housing program was the primary federal vehicle for improving the housing of the poor. In 1949 a new form of housing subsidy was created in the urban renewal program. While urban renewal had many purposes, most of them beyond the scope of this study, it was in part a means of bringing down the cost of building new housing.[13] It accomplished this by employing the power of eminent domain (again, by local government agencies) to acquire urban land; the buildings were then razed and the land was resold at auction to private developers. The subsidy thus took the form of

---

[11] U.S. Department of Housing and Urban Development, *1967 HUD Statistical Yearbook,* 1969, pp. 258–64.

[12] Housing and Urban Development Act of 1965, P. L. 89–117, Sec. 103(a). The program is known as "Section 23" because Section 103(a) was technically an amendment to the U.S. Housing Act of 1937, and created the leased housing program as Section 23 of the 1937 act.

[13] Urban renewal is reviewed in detail in Jerome Rothenberg, *Economic Evaluation of Urban Renewal* (Washington, D.C.: Brookings Institution, 1967); and John C. Weicher, *Urban Renewal: National Program for Local Problems* (Washington, D.C.: American Enterprise Institute for Public Policy Research, 1972).

a partial write-down of land costs. Since land typically represents only about 20 to 25 percent of the cost of a new housing unit, this partial subsidy was not an efficient device for bringing down housing costs, particularly for the poor, and in fact the program came under intense criticism, particularly after 1960, for its perverse income redistribution effects: it demolished housing for the poor and replaced it with housing for the rich, or at least the upper half of the income distribution. Congress increased its efforts to redirect the program toward assisting the poor.

Urban renewal was also attacked for razing significant numbers of standard housing units along with substandard ones in the same neighborhoods. This criticism led to an emphasis on rehabilitation of existing units which had its beginnings in the late 1950s but became particularly strong during the mid-1960s. Relatively little actual rehabilitation was carried out, however.

In 1973, the entire program was finally suspended by President Nixon and replaced with a Community Development Block Grant program (CDBG) providing local governments with funds which they could use either for urban renewal projects of their own choosing or for a variety of other purposes such as construction of water and sewer facilities, development of public parks, and other public works. In the first three years of the grants there was a decline in the relative share of funds spent on slum clearance and redevelopment, the traditional form of urban renewal, and an increasing emphasis on housing rehabilitation and local public works.[14] The rehabilitation activities in particular have been concentrated in middle-income neighborhoods.

Federal concern that not enough of the CDBG funds were being spent in the worst neighborhoods led to the creation in 1977 of the Urban Development Action Grants program (UDAG) as a supplement to the CDBG program. HUD awards funds at its discretion for specific local redevelopment projects proposed by cities. This is the project selection and funding system used for urban renewal, and some of the first UDAG projects are located in renewal areas; thus, the original program may be reenacted under another name.

Interest Subsidies

At about the same time that public housing was established, Congress created the Federal Housing Administration (FHA), with the intent

---

[14] U.S. Department of Housing and Urban Development, *Community Development Block Grant Program: Third Annual Report,* 1978.

of increasing homeownership. FHA insured long-term self-amortizing home mortgages for middle-income families. Such mortgages were something of an innovation in the 1930s. At that time the typical mortgage ran for ten years or less and required payment of interest only during its life, leaving the buyer with a "balloon payment" at the end. FHA mortgages also required low down payments and carried a low interest rate. The insurance was offered as an inducement to private lenders to make such loans, and insurance claims were paid from premiums charged to the home buyer.[15]

The significance of FHA for the development of housing subsidies was that the system was widely perceived as a success—much more so than public housing. The rate of homeownership increased dramatically in the 1940s and has continued to rise, and the insurance program proved actuarially sound, with premium payments more than covering default losses and administrative costs.

FHA also insured rental apartment buildings under several smaller programs. About 825,000 new apartments had been insured before 1960. In this area FHA was somewhat less successful, since the largest program, providing the most generous insurance coverage (Section 608), had been plagued by scandals and terminated in the 1950s. Nevertheless, the basic apartment insurance program dating back to 1937 was regarded as effective.

Until 1961 the FHA insurance programs and public housing proceeded on separate tracks and were administered by separate agencies. In that year a new program was created in an attempt to bring the benefits of FHA insurance to lower-income families: this was the Section 221 (d) (3) BMIR (below market interest rate) program. (Most housing programs are known by the numbers of the sections of the National Housing Act which created them, probably because the English language is not rich in synonyms for "mortgage interest rate subsidy.") Under this program FHA would insure mortgages on apartment projects which were to be owned by nonprofit sponsors or limited dividend corporations if the mortgages carried below-market interest rates. The lower rate and the absence of profit were to be reflected in lower rents, making the apartments affordable by the target "moderate-income" population—those who were too well off to be eligible for public housing but too poor to take advantage of the FHA homeownership program or to afford the rents of unsubsidized new apartment projects. Dollar mortgage limits per apartment were also written into the statute so as to confine the program to the desired clientele. Although both newly constructed and previously existing

---

[15] FHA is discussed in greater detail in chapter 7.

apartment projects were eligible, the program was intended in part to stimulate the housing construction industry, which was then in the midst of a cyclical downturn, and in fact 90 percent of the units subsidized by the program were new.

To induce private lenders to write mortgages at below-market rates the Federal National Mortgage Association (FNMA) was empowered to buy the loans from the originators at face value. (FNMA had been created in 1938 as a secondary market facility for FHA-insured mortgages, with the power of borrowing funds in order to buy the mortgages from their originators. The theory behind this was that it could draw funds from geographic areas where savings were high in relation to mortgage demand and buy mortgages in areas where savings were low.)[16] The interest rate was first tied to the federal borrowing rate, but in 1965 it was set at a flat 3 percent. The net effect of this complicated arrangement was that FNMA lent money at below-market interest rates to private sponsors to build moderate-income housing.

Rent Supplement Program. The 1961 legislation also created a Section 221 (d) (3) "market rate" program, which extended FHA insurance to apartment project mortgages with longer terms and lower down payments than had been customary. The apartments built under this program were not originally subsidized, but in 1965 Congress enacted a rent supplement program, under which the federal government could make rental payments on behalf of tenants to the sponsors of Section 221 (d) (3) projects. This permitted very low-income families, similar to those in public housing, to live in the unsubsidized market rate projects.

The rent supplement program represented a notable departure in policy because the subsidy was based on the income of the tenant, with the federal government paying the difference between 25 percent of income and the rental value of the apartment. Previous subsidies under public housing, urban renewal, and Section 221 (d) (3) had been tied to the cost of the unit. If a family could not then afford the subsidized unit from its own resources, it did not receive special assistance. (The 25 percent of income limit for public housing tenants was enacted later, in 1969.)

---

[16] The role of FNMA in the American housing finance system is described in Milton P. Semer et al., "Evolution of Federal Legislative Policy in Housing: Housing Credits," in National Housing Policy Review, *Housing in the Seventies: Working Papers*, vol. 1, pp. 3–81; and in Patric H. Hendershott and Kevin E. Villani, *Regulation and Reform of the Housing Finance System* (Washington, D.C.: American Enterprise Institute for Public Policy Research, 1978), p. 206.

The program excited great political controversy at the time. It was limited to certain population categories, such as the elderly and veterans, but since one category was "those living in substandard housing," without further definition, the restriction was not very "restrictive."

Program Limitations. Section 221 (d) (3) had a relatively short history. Its budget impact was very large, since each mortgage purchased by FNMA showed up dollar for dollar as a federal budget outlay. This was a kind of budgetary illusion. FNMA would receive payment of principal and interest from the mortgagor over the life of the mortgage, so that the present value of the budget outlay was the difference between the initial purchase price and the value of the monthly mortgage payments, discounted at the higher market interest rate rather than at the lower subsidized rate at which the mortgage was issued. The subsidy thus was essentially the difference between a forty-year stream of payments capitalized at perhaps 5 to 6 percent and the same payments capitalized at the 3 percent subsidized interest rate. But in the accounting of the federal budget, the face value of the mortgage was recorded as an outlay in the initial year, with a very small offsetting receipt, and the resulting large one-year deficit made the program politically vulnerable.

Other factors contributed to its vulnerability. The interest rate subsidy proved to be insufficient to bring the below-market interest rate apartments within the financial means of most "moderate-income" families. In 1968 the National Commission on Urban Problems, headed by former Senator Paul Douglas (D–Ill.), noted that most of the units located in urban renewal projects were "actually designed for those in the upper ranges of the moderate-income category."[17] At the same time, rent supplements effectively served the same income group that public housing served.[18] Moreover, the subsidy did not prove large enough to bring about a substantial volume of construction; in the first seven years of the program only 73,000 apartments were started, less than 10 percent of total multifamily production. The program thus had missed its targets despite enormous budget outlays, and it was superseded in 1968 by Section 236, another program combining interest rate subsidies with FHA insurance.

Section 236. The new program provided a large subsidy at lower

---

[17] National Commission on Urban Problems, *Building the American City* (New York: Praeger, 1969), p. 163.
[18] National Housing Policy Review, *Housing in the Seventies*, 1974, table 23, p. 120, and table 30, p. 128.

budget impact by paying the subsidy annually to the project owner, rather than buying the mortgage outright and thus paying the entire principal amount immediately. In this respect the subsidy mechanism was similar to that used for public housing. It differed, however, in that the mortgage was to be issued by the lender at the going market interest rate. The federal government would then pay the difference between the monthly mortgage payment needed to amortize this mortgage and the amount needed to amortize the mortgage at a lower interest rate, down to 1 percent. The precise amount of the subsidy depended on the income of the tenant; the subsidy therefore was conditioned on income, with a maximum determined by the 1 percent interest rate. (This subsidy mechanism had been recommended for public housing by Frances Perkins, secretary of labor at the time that program was enacted.)

Section 236 also continued the rent supplement program directly for those families that still could not afford the apartments, making both moderate- and low-income families eligible for assistance. As was the case with Section 221, mortgage limits were established and the program was open to both new and existing apartments, but, again, 90 percent of those subsidized were new.

Tax Shelter. Section 236 projects, like those in the previous interest subsidy program, could be owned by private nonprofit or limited dividend sponsors. Financial incentives for private ownership were afforded by the advantageous tax treatment available to individual investors in the projects. The most important inducement was the ability of the owners to depreciate the project more rapidly for tax purposes than its actual decline in economic value would warrant. An investor could then deduct this accelerated depreciation from his or her income, paying tax only on that amount of income in excess of the project depreciation (and other deductions and exclusions). Thus, income from other sources could be "sheltered" from taxation, even though the investor in fact incurred no cash outlays and suffered no out-of-pocket loss as a result of the depreciation.

The dollar value of the excess depreciation was subject to recapture as tax revenue when the project was sold, but if the project were held for ten years the excess depreciation would be taxed as capital gains rather than ordinary income, even though the depreciation had originally been used to shelter ordinary income.

Accelerated depreciation for apartment projects and other buildings was enacted in 1954 as part of a general effort to spur private investment; at the time, congressional attention was focused on machinery and business equipment rather than on housing.

Before 1961 the tax advantages of FHA-insured projects were available only to corporations, because only corporations could own insured projects. In the Housing Acts of 1961 and 1964,[19] however, "limited partnerships" were allowed to own projects. This change was desired by both FHA and the project developers, who shared a desire to encourage construction of FHA-insured rental housing. It was not especially intended to stimulate subsidized housing production.

In a limited partnership each investor is liable only for the amount he invests—rather than for the entire project, as with the traditional unlimited partnership. The value of limited partnerships as tax shelters was greatly enhanced in a 1947 Supreme Court case, *Crane v. Commissioner of Internal Revenue*,[20] in which the court ruled that an investor could deduct depreciation not only up to the amount of his own personal investment but also including his proportionate share of the amount borrowed by the partnership, for which he is not individually liable. For example, if a project cost $1 million and had a $900,000 mortgage, then a limited partner investing $10,000 (10 percent of the partnership's equity in the project) could claim depreciation of up to $100,000 (10 percent of the value of the project). In housing especially, with mortgages representing by far the largest source of funds for a project, this ruling conferred substantial tax benefits, once the law permitted limited partnerships to own projects.[21]

Tax law changes in 1969 provided further stimulus for housing investment generally and for Section 236 in particular. The Tax Reform Act of that year reduced the amount of accelerated depreciation available for investments other than housing, thus giving housing investment a comparative advantage.[22] After this change the number of publicly offered real estate tax shelters nearly quadrupled from 1970 to 1972, and their total dollar value more than tripled.[23] Richard Slitor has estimated that the 1969 law diverted about $1.2 billion in investment from nonresidential structures to housing, representing 60,000 to 80,000 apartments.[24] The law gave a further advantage to

---

[19] Housing Act of 1961, P. L. 87–70, Sec. 607(l); Housing Act of 1964, P. L. 88–560, Sec. 114(a).

[20] 331 U.S. 1 (1947).

[21] This description is not intended as a full discussion of the tax treatment of investment in rental housing, but rather as a brief explanation of the major provisions that affected the development of subsidized projects. For more extensive discussion, see National Housing Policy Review, *Housing in the Seventies*, chap. 2; and U.S. Congressional Budget Office, *Real Estate Tax Shelter Subsidies and Direct Subsidy Alternatives*, 1977, chap. 2.

[22] Tax Reform Act of 1969, P. L. 91–172.

[23] Congressional Budget Office, *Real Estate Tax Shelter Subsidies*, p. 28.

[24] Richard E. Slitor, "Rationale of the Present Tax Benefits for Homeownership," in National Housing Policy Review, *Housing in the Seventies: Working Papers*, vol. 2, p. 940.

subsidized projects by leaving unchanged the holding period for avoiding recapture while lengthening it to 16⅔ years for unsubsidized apartment buildings. While this was a small advantage, it was the first time the tax laws had specifically favored subsidized projects. By far the larger share of tax sheltered projects were unsubsidized, however, despite this change.

Program Activity. With tax advantages to developers and owners, and with large subsidies to tenants, Section 236 made a rapid start. By 1971 more apartments had been built under it than had been built during the entire Section 221 (d) (3) BMIR program. Section 236 was also more successful in reaching its target income group. As of 1972, more than half the subsidy recipients had incomes between $4,000 and $7,000, with a median of $5,300, nearly double that for public housing occupants.[25] (Since that time real income of participants in both programs seems to be declining.) There have been other differences in the clienteles; Section 236 tenants have tended to be somewhat younger, and a higher proportion of them are employed.

Homeownership Subsidies

Parallel to the policy changes for apartments during the 1960s, a series of programs to encourage homeownership for lower-income families was also being enacted. These programs began in 1961 with Section 221 (d) (2), which provided mortgage insurance without subsidy for longer-term, lower down payment loans, to riskier borrowers, than had heretofore been eligible. As with the original FHA program, this was used extensively to buy existing homes: about 60,000 new homes and 300,000 existing ones were insured during the 1960s.

In 1968 Section 235 introduced subsidies for home purchase on the same formula as the Section 236 program. No down payment was required; in fact, the mortgage was typically for a larger amount than the sales price, to cover closing costs. The buyer spent about $100 as his or her share of closing costs and was then entitled to move in. Mortgage limits were set well below the prices of typical homes then being built. The limits ranged from $15,000 to $20,000 at first, compared with a median new home price of over $25,000 in 1969.

Like its counterpart, Section 236, Section 235 grew quickly, with over 300,000 new homes and 80,000 existing ones subsidized during the first four years of the program. Concurrently with the expansion

---

[25] National Housing Policy Review, *Housing in the Seventies*, table 17, p. 113.

of Sections 235 and 236, unsubsidized housing production boomed in the early 1970s. Total starts reached over 2.3 million in 1972.

Section 235 served a slightly higher income group than Section 236 but a markedly lower group than were customarily homeowners. The median income of households in the program was $6,500 in 1972, compared with a median for all owners of $10,400 in 1969.[26] Most families were young with two or three children. The program had a strong geographical concentration in the South and West, where construction costs and home prices were generally lower, so that more of these families might have bought homes without the subsidy than the difference in nominal income would suggest. It seems clear, however, that they were on balance significantly worse off financially than the usual home buyer. The homes they bought were generally much smaller, with fewer amenities, than the typical new home being built at the time.

Programs and Problems in the Early 1970s

By the end of 1972 there were three main housing programs: low-rent public housing for the poorest, Section 236 for renters with slightly higher income, and the Section 235 "homeownership for the poor" program, serving a still slightly higher income group. Urban renewal, while a broader program, was also producing housing, albeit largely for much higher income groups. (There were also an enormous variety of programs for special population groups, such as the elderly, veterans, and American Indians, and for special types of housing, such as nursing homes and mobile homes. Most of these have been quite small and have rung minor changes on the mechanisms used in the programs already described. The largest is the Section 502 program of the Farmers Home Administration within the Department of Agriculture, providing "235-like" subsidies for new homes in rural areas.)[27]

By the end of 1972 all of the major programs had run into serious problems of one sort or another. Most visibly, scandals had occurred in several areas, particularly among Section 235 existing homes. Inexpensive houses of low quality were bought by real estate "speculators," who made cosmetic improvements and then bribed FHA inspectors to certify that the houses were meeting the quality stand-

---

[26] Ibid., table 14, p. 107.
[27] Critical reviews of Section 502 are contained in Henry J. Aaron, *Shelter and Subsidies* (Washington, D.C.: Brookings Institution, 1972), chap. 9; and National Housing Policy Review, *Housing in the Seventies*, pp. 128–35.

ards of the program.[28] The homes were then sold to eligible families whose mortgages were insured by the federal government. Often the homes soon needed major repairs which the new owners could not afford. When this happened the rational decision for the owner was frequently to abandon the house. In effect, the owner would behave as if he or she were a renter, treating the $100 "down payment" as a security deposit and ignoring the minuscule equity built up in the home in the first few months of the thirty-year mortgage.

Abandonment was also widespread in other areas, unaccompanied by scandal, because the economic incentives to abandon a home existed also for families who experienced job loss or transfer within a year or two of moving in. Their equity in the home was typically less than the cost of selling it.

The subsidy formula inadvertently compounded the problem. It diminished the incentive for many buyers to be concerned with quality. They were required to pay 20 percent of their income, or the amount needed to amortize the mortgage at 1 percent, whichever was higher. For those paying by income, an increase in house price, whether representing higher quality or not, did not affect their payment but simply raised the subsidy. This threw more of the burden of making the program work on HUD staff and less on market forces, and probably contributed to the program abuses. In addition, the formula was perverse when operating costs increased. The family receiving the maximum subsidy, paying off the mortgage at 1 percent, had to meet cost increases from its own resources, while the higher-income families paying 20 percent of income would have the subsidy raised to cover all cost increases until the 1 percent limit was reached.

The abandonment of homes that it had subsidized embarrassed the federal government; FHA insurance turned abandonment into a financial problem. Mortgage insurance provides a market test of housing programs that is relatively rare among government activities. The middle-income programs had passed that test and proved themselves profitable, but the subsidized programs failed it. Sections 235 and 236, like Sections 221 (d) (2) and (d) (3) before them, were proving to be actuarially unsound. Actual defaults were high and projected defaults exceeded the value of the mortgage insurance premiums. The results of the failure were becoming obvious in the early 1970s. It was increasingly likely that the insurance funds for the subsidized

---

[28] U.S. Congress, House, Committee on Banking and Currency, *Investigation and Hearing of Abuses in Federal Low- and Moderate-Income Housing Programs*, 91st Cong., 2nd sess., December 1970; U.S. Congress, House, Committee on Banking and Currency, *Interim Report on HUD Investigation of Low- and Moderate-Income Housing Programs*, 92nd Cong., 1st sess., March 31, 1971.

housing programs would be unable to meet the claims upon them and Congress would have to appropriate funds to pay off the defaulted mortgages. This raised the program costs markedly.

While the scandals of Section 235 had attracted the greatest amount of public attention, the apartment subsidy programs were in fact incurring higher defaults. A subsequent analysis by the U.S. General Accounting Office found that default rates were much higher among the nonprofit sponsors than among the limited partnerships.[29] One reason for the difference may have been that the tenants in the former projects had much lower incomes.[30] As with Section 235, the subsidy formula was perverse in that tenants had to pay the higher of either 25 percent of the income or a "basic rent" consisting of operating costs and the amount needed to amortize the mortgage at a 1 percent interest rate. When operating costs rose, the basic rent rose, and the poorest tenants had to meet the increase out of their own incomes while HUD raised the subsidy for those paying 25 percent of their income.

The limited partnership projects were also criticized on the grounds that they were attracting investors with no knowledge of or interest in housing who were concerned solely with the tax shelter.[31] Private ownership of subsidized housing had been advocated as a means of promoting better management and maintenance, but the tax incentives were largely unrelated to the operating experience of the project. Some analysts went further and argued that the tax incentives in fact discouraged maintenance because they encouraged rapid turnover of ownership.[32] In fact, the tax shelter does create some incentive for at least minimally adequate maintenance, because much of the tax benefit is lost if the project goes into default in the first ten years; the accelerated depreciation would be recaptured as ordinary income in that case, as with a sale of the project.[33] This does not necessarily encourage good maintenance, however, and one study indicates that management performance has been somewhat worse on the average in tax shelter projects than in other low-income developments.[34]

---

[29] U.S. General Accounting Office, Comptroller General, *Section 236 Rental Housing: An Evaluation with Lessons for the Future*, 1978.

[30] National Housing Policy Review, *Housing in the Seventies*, pp. 112–13.

[31] Congressional Budget Office, *Real Estate Tax Shelter Subsidies*, p. 64, n. 76.

[32] Paul Taubman, "Housing and Income Tax Subsidies," in National Housing Policy Review, *Housing in the Seventies: Working Papers*, vol. 2, pp. 982–98, especially p. 991.

[33] Congressional Budget Office, *Real Estate Tax Shelter Subsidies*, pp. 53–55.

[34] Morton Isler, Robert Sadacca, and Margaret Drury, *Keys to Successful Housing Management* (Washington, D.C.: The Urban Institute, 1974).

Default and abandonment created still further problems for the federal government and for the cities and neighborhoods in which the housing was located. After paying off the mortgage, HUD would acquire title to a house or apartment and would then offer it for sale, as had been the practice since 1937. Before 1960 the housing acquired by HUD could usually be resold without great difficulty. But with the advent of mortgage insurance for subsidized housing, defaults had increased dramatically and the rate of resale had not kept pace. The inventory of HUD-held unsold homes rose from 27,000 in 1960 to 62,000 in 1969 and then to 149,000 by 1972. The inventory of apartments went from 4,000 in 1960 to 54,000 in 1972.

HUD found that it could not sell these units at prices close to the original amount of the insured mortgage. Sale at a lower price was an admission of error and also appeared in the budget as an expenditure of the difference between insurance amount and sale price in the year of sale. But holding a house off the market until the full mortgage amount could be recouped generated continuing—albeit smaller—outlays for protection and management. Moreover, a vacant house created problems for the neighborhood. Despite efforts to avert it, vandalism was frequent enough to bring complaints from neighbors. In some cities (for example, in Detroit), where large numbers of homes in a given neighborhood had been subsidized, abandoned vacant units were often concentrated in the neighborhood, making it less safe for the remaining residents and thus encouraging further abandonment.

(A number of programs designed to sell these homes and apartment projects have been attempted. The best known is probably "Urban Homesteading," in which abandoned homes are given "as is" to families, often chosen by lottery, who agree to move in, make repairs to bring the homes up to standard, and live in them for a fixed number of years. The program has attracted wide attention since it was begun locally in Philadelphia and Wilmington in the early 1970s. From the standpoint of HUD's property disposition, it is a politically acceptable recognition of the fact that the houses have close to zero market value in their current condition.)

While the housing programs were beset with problems, the budget implications of even a successful program were becoming clearer and less attractive. The subsidy per unit under Section 235 or 236 might be only one-thirtieth of the subsidy under Section 221 in the first year, but the newer programs were ten times as large and, since subsidies continued on units originally assisted in the past, the outlays grew rapidly from year to year.

At the same time the older programs of urban renewal and public housing continued to come under criticism—the former for destroy-ing neighborhoods and hurting low-income families, the latter be-cause a number of projects in various cities were beset by crime and other problems. Overall occupancy rates were high, but some projects were so undesirable that they had high vacancies despite the large subsidies received by tenants. The most spectacular "problem proj-ect" was the Pruitt-Igoe development in St. Louis. This had been opened in the mid-1950s and had been widely praised at the time, but by 1971 it was largely vacant and vandalized, and the city of St. Louis and HUD concluded that much of it should be razed.[35] Dem-olition of three buildings in 1972 attracted national attention and became a symbol of all that was wrong with public housing.

Section 8

During 1972 there was increasing political recognition of the fact that the housing programs were not working as desired. There was con-siderable discussion of alternatives, which culminated on January 8, 1973, when President Nixon abruptly and unexpectedly suspended all the housing programs and announced that he was setting up a task force, the National Housing Policy Review (NHPR), to study the programs and make recommendations.

The NHPR task force proposed a major policy shift to a "demand-side" subsidy given directly to the family, rather than the customary "supply-side" subsidies tied to specific housing units, which had been the standard pattern. The demand-side subsidy could be used for either new or existing housing. To implement this policy the task force recommended adapting and expanding the leased public hous-ing program. Its recommendations were enacted in 1974, and the revised Section 23 program became Section 8 of the 1974 Housing and Community Development Act.[36]

Section 8 differed from Section 23 in several ways. Families with incomes of up to 80 percent of the local median—well above most public housing income limits—were eligible for assistance. The sub-sidy was given to the household in the form of a commitment by the federal government to pay part of the household's rent. The recipient could then use the entitlement to seek his or her own housing, ne-gotiating a rental agreement with the landlord. The housing had to meet certain quality standards that were to be defined in detail by the local public housing authority, which would administer the pro-

---

[35] Wolf von Eckhardt, "Death of the City of the Future," *Washington Post*, June 24, 1972.
[36] Housing and Community Development Act of 1974, P. L. 93–383.

gram on the local level. The federal government would pay the subsidy to the local agency, which would in turn pay the landlord.

The subsidy formula was also an innovation. It paid the difference between the rent on a standard quality apartment or house in a particular locality (called the fair market rent, or FMR) and 25 percent of the recipient's income. The FMR, and thus the subsidy, varied with family size. The recipient was given some financial incentive to seek housing renting for less than the FMR, in the form of a direct payment of part of the difference. Units renting for more than the FMR, however, were ineligible for the program, so that the recipient was limited in choice. The household could not spend more than 25 percent of its own income for rent and could not rent a unit better than those available at the FMR. Another novel feature was that low-income tenants living in standard quality housing (renting for no more than the FMR) but paying more than 25 percent of their income for rent could receive a subsidy while remaining in their current residence. This provision recognized the fact that much existing housing was in standard condition according to the customary definitions, and that the housing problems of most low-income families were financial.

The subsidy mechanism for new apartment projects was more like that used in the early supply-side programs. Private developers and state housing agencies were expected to propose constructing projects which would meet established quality standards. HUD would then approve certain projects, promising to subsidize tenants on the same basis as in existing housing. The sponsor was guaranteed the fair market rent on all occupied units for a period of twenty years. Higher FMRs were set for new projects to reflect construction costs rather than actual rents for standard quality housing. FHA insurance was also available but was not automatic: projects could be assisted without being insured.

Section 8 was thus partly a pure income transfer and partly a housing subsidy of the traditional type. For tenants subsidized in place it was an income transfer; for tenants of new projects it was much like conventional public housing. For those who used their subsidy to move from one existing house or apartment to another, the housing quality standards imposed limits on the extent to which the program was simply an income transfer; some at least might be induced to live in better housing than they would have chosen with an unrestricted cash payment.

Like Sections 235 and 236 before it, Section 8 made a quick start. The existing program, in particular, was able to begin subsidizing tenants during 1975, and by the end of 1976 over 110,000 were being assisted, more than double the number in the first two years of the Section 235 and Section 236 existing programs combined.[37] New construction proceeded more slowly, but by the end of September 1977 some 135,000 apartments had been started, about two-thirds as many as in the first three years of Section 236.[38]

Section 8 served the same low-income groups that public housing and rent supplements served. In mid-1976 the median income of subsidy recipients was estimated at $3,800. About 25 percent of the households reported receiving some wage income; 70 percent had a female head. Minorities were participating roughly in proportion to their share of the eligible population, and most households contained only one or two persons.[39]

Policy since 1974

Even as Section 8 was starting, housing policy was beginning to shift back toward emphasizing new construction. Housing starts had been dropping since 1973, and in 1975 the lowest level of production since 1946 was recorded. In addition, President Nixon's suspension of the older programs in 1973 was being challenged in Congress and the courts as a violation of the constitutional power of Congress to appropriate money. At the beginning of 1976, therefore, the Section 235 program was revived in a modified form, using funds appropriated but not spent before January 1973. The program was limited to newly constructed homes only, and the maximum subsidy was set at the difference between the mortgage payment at the market interest rate and the mortgage payment at a 5 percent (instead of a 1 percent) rate. The revised program was therefore aimed at a higher income group than the original. Later in 1976, Congress reactivated the traditional public housing construction program, mandating that part of the funds requested for Section 8 (itself technically a public housing program) be used for conventional new construction.

---

[37] U.S. Office of the President, *Ninth Annual Report on the National Housing Goal*, 95th Cong., 1st sess., January 1977, p. 7.

[38] "Sec. 8 Data Have HUD Brass Smiling," *Housing Affairs Letter,* October 7, 1977, pp. 3–4.

[39] U.S. Department of Housing and Urban Development, Office of Policy Development and Research, "A Report to the Secretary on the Section 8 Existing Housing Program" (unpublished), June 30, 1976, p. 6. Data for 1977 are available for a few characteristics; they are consistent with those cited in the text (U.S. Department of Housing and Urban Development, *1977 HUD Statistical Yearbook,* pp. 264–97). Only income data are available for Section 8 tenants for 1978. The median income for those in existing housing was about $3,800, compared with $3,700 for public housing and $3,500 for those receiving rent supplements.

There was renewed interest in the Section 221 financing mechanism, with an important budgetary modification: lenders were to provide funds at below-market rates of interest and could then sell the mortgages to the Government National Mortgage Association (GNMA) at face value. (GNMA had been the successor in this regard to FNMA since 1968.) GNMA, however, was then to resell the mortgages at the market price. The net effect was that GNMA bought a 7.5 percent mortgage and sold it at a discount reflecting the higher market rate. The budget impact consisted only of the difference between the purchase price and the sale price, which was roughly proportional to the interest rate difference. This device had been used to stimulate production during the 1974 and 1975 housing recession; it was known as the Tandem Plan, because GNMA was in effect pairing sellers and buyers of mortgages. As an antirecession measure, no limit had been placed on home purchase price or buyer income, but in 1976 the Tandem Plan was authorized for use with new Section 8 projects to bring down the interest rate and thus to bring down the subsidy payment.[40] It had been used to a minor extent with Section 236 for the same purpose.

Since President Carter took office the trend has continued. In his final budget President Ford proposed a "modified block grant" approach for Section 8. Localities would be promised a specific dollar subsidy amount and could choose to subsidize either new or existing units instead of being assigned a given number in each category. This plan is somewhat similar to the Community Development Block Grant. It was not adopted by the incoming administration.[41]

Early in 1977 advocates of welfare reform proposed incorporating housing subsidies into their scheme, creating an unrestricted income transfer in lieu of all current programs. HUD vigorously opposed this, and it was not part of the president's welfare proposal. Instead, his first budget contained an expansion of the Section 8 new construction program and a modification of the existing program to require the upgrading of all dwellings, regardless of their original quality, as a condition of eligibility. These changes had the effect of emphasizing housing construction and employment once again and reducing the use of the existing stock to house the poor.

In addition, during the past two years the revised Section 235 program has been liberalized, although production under either revised version has been very small. In early 1978 the General Ac-

---

[40] U.S. Congress, Senate, Committee on Banking, Housing, and Urban Affairs, *Housing Amendments of 1976*, 94th Cong., 2nd sess., April 12, 1976, p. 5.
[41] Block grants are discussed more fully in chapter 5.

counting Office recommended reviving Section 236, though this has so far not occurred.

At this writing, therefore, the panoply of programs is much like that of 1972 before the moratorium, and the similarity may increase. This situation suggests that a knowledge of past programs may contribute to an understanding of housing policy in the near future.

4

Current Subsidy Programs

At present there are three major programs that provide housing assistance for low-income households: public housing; Section 8 new construction; and Section 8 existing housing. This chapter describes the ways in which these programs operate and the problems they are currently encountering. It also briefly reviews two smaller variants of Section 8, the "substantial rehabilitation" and "loan management and property disposition" programs, but omits various minor programs (for example, Indian housing).

Public Housing

Public housing is the oldest and largest housing program for the poor; indeed, it is the only major current program which has been in operation for more than five years. In the public mind it probably typifies federal housing programs; it has attracted far more popular discussion and academic analysis than any other program, and the demolition in 1972 of the Pruitt-Igoe public housing project (mentioned in the previous chapter) has symbolized the failure of federal housing policy in general to many critics. Public housing has significantly influenced all subsequent housing subsidy programs, including Section 8, which was explicitly designed to replace it.

The development of the public housing program has been traced, and its workings described, in the previous chapter. It was revived by Congress in 1976 in essentially the same form and is the only one of the suspended subsidy programs to be so reactivated. (The Section 235 homeownership assistance program, revived by President Ford in the same year, was substantially modified to serve a different clientele and a somewhat different purpose; this program is discussed in chapter 7.)

There are some differences between the present public housing program and its original operation. Under the present program local authorities are expected to buy projects designed by private developers (the Turnkey method) rather than designing their own; special permission from the U.S. Department of Housing and Urban Development (HUD) is required for the latter production technique. The fund allocation mechanism has also been changed by Congress. Subsidies are available to localities in accordance with a formula reflecting population, poverty, substandard housing, and the rental vacancy rate, rather than being awarded by the federal government at its discretion to specific projects proposed by local authorities. The same allocation formula is used for Section 8.

Since the program was revived, Congress has appropriated funds to finance between 30,000 and 50,000 new or rehabilitated units annually, which is about as many as were built in a typical year during the 1950s and 1960s.[1] HUD approved 23,000 for construction in fiscal year 1977 and about double that in each of the next two years. It anticipates approvals of 30,000 to 40,000 annually through 1981. Actual construction, however, has lagged far behind appropriations and approvals. Only 5,400 units were started in fiscal 1977 and only 6,700 in fiscal 1978; HUD had expected more than 20,000 in each year. Starts rose in 1979 to 22,000, and further sharp increases are projected for both 1980 and 1981. Completions have been on a par with starts.

Obviously, the program has proceeded quite slowly, although the pace may be quickening. A possible explanation is that Turnkey projects are initiated by private developers, who may be unwilling to participate in the program; another suggestion is that local authorities have lost many of the personnel with the skills to develop projects in the years since President Nixon's moratorium.[2] (To expedite projects, HUD is now planning to train local agency staff.) Neither of these explanations is entirely convincing. Authorities can request waivers of the Turnkey requirement if local developers are not interested in the program; furthermore, there has been a substantial volume of reservations, meaning that HUD has approved particular projects. And it seems unlikely that the development skills

---

[1] U.S. Department of Housing and Urban Development, *Summary of the HUD Budget, Fiscal Year 1981*, January 1980, p. H–1. Unless otherwise noted, data on activity in current programs are taken from the *HUD Budget Summary* for various years. Information on program activity is summarized in exhibit VI of the summary table section of each year's summary.

[2] "Public Housing Chief Wants Boosts in Program's Productive Capacity," *Housing Affairs Letter*, January 19, 1979, p. 5.

built up in thirty-five years could be so entirely dissipated in five, or that they are so exceptionally difficult to acquire.

An alternative explanation for the slow pace at which the program is proceeding is that public housing projects are now subject to a variety of federal requirements that were absent or were unimportant before 1973. In recent years housing programs have increasingly been required—either by Congress or administratively—to serve purposes that are additional to the basic objective of helping low-income families. These "social goals" include equal opportunity in construction employment; care for the environment; and metropolitan areawide planning. Projects must be reviewed by area planning agencies (the A-95 review process) and the government of the locality in which they will be built. These reviews are intended to assure conformity with local plans as well as to encourage areawide planning. The local and metropolitan plans and objectives can of course conflict; if they do the development process takes longer. Environmental impact reviews for housing projects appear to go beyond the requirements of the Environmental Protection Act, covering projects of all sizes.[3]

The High Cost of Public Housing. Such requirements as those listed above not only take time; they add to cost—and the public housing program is quite costly. The budget for fiscal year 1981 projects an average construction cost of $57,000 per unit.[4] This is not far below the median new home price of $63,000 in 1979, though inflation between 1979 and 1981 will increase the difference. Public housing construction has always been a relatively expensive way to provide housing for the poor, in large part because of legislative or administrative regulations aimed at secondary objectives; in a sense, the current social goals are merely the latest in a series of such regulations.

Probably the most important single factor increasing the cost of construction is the Davis-Bacon Act.[5] This legislation requires that federal construction projects (including subsidized housing) pay the "prevailing scale" in the local area to all construction workers. The act was passed in 1931, during the depression, as an attempt to prevent out-of-town contractors from underbidding local firms by

---

[3] "Sec. 8 Environmental Review Upheld," ibid., p. 4.
[4] Data on public housing costs are taken from U.S. Office of Management and Budget, *The Budget of the United States, Fiscal Year 1981*, 1980.
[5] P. L. 71–798. Recent major studies of the Davis-Bacon Act include: John P. Gould, *Davis-Bacon Act: The Economics of Prevailing Wage Laws* (Washington, D.C.: American Enterprise Institute for Public Policy Research, 1971), and Armand J. Thieblot, Jr., *The Davis-Bacon Act* (Philadelphia: The Wharton School, Industrial Research Unit, 1975).

bringing in their own work forces. It was a sectional and even a racial measure: northern firms were concerned that southern contractors were underbidding them on northern contracts with "cheap colored labor."[6] This measure was also strongly supported by organized labor.

Determination of prevailing wages is made by the U.S. Department of Labor, which has primarily used union wage rates as prevailing wages. Most apartment buildings in the United States are built by union labor, so this in itself would not raise the cost of public housing. However, a substantial share of the union rates established by the Labor Department as prevailing do not in fact apply in the locality of the construction project. One study made in the 1960s estimated that from 25 to 38 percent of building projects had established wage rates that were taken from noncontiguous counties, at an average distance of seventy to eighty miles from the construction site.[7]

The effect of Davis-Bacon on housing project costs is substantial. The U.S. General Accounting Office studied twenty-eight projects and concluded that construction costs were increased by 10 percent as a result of improper administration of the act (that is, setting wages above the local rate).[8] There is some evidence that the actual estimate may have been much higher than this figure.[9] The General Accounting Office conclusions, however, indicate greater costs than do private studies. For example, Goldfarb and Morrall found that Davis-Bacon wage determinations were generally *below* union and even average wages in the area by about 2 to 5 percent. They attribute this surprising result to lags in the process of making the determinations. After adjusting for the lags they conclude that savings of about 1.5 to 2 percent of construction costs could be achieved by using average rather than union wages.[10] Their estimate of the dollar savings is similar to that of Armand Thieblot.[11]

A second factor that has contributed to the high cost of public housing is the traditional practice of building it on expensive land in large cities. Public housing was originally tied to slum clearance as

[6] Thieblot, *Davis-Bacon Act*, p. 9.
[7] Damodar Gujarati, "The Economics of the Davis-Bacon Act" (Ph.D. dissertation, University of Chicago, 1965), pp. 48–62.
[8] U.S. General Accounting Office, Comptroller General, *Need for Improved Administration of the Davis-Bacon Act Noted over a Decade of General Accounting Office Reviews*, 1971, pp. 9–10.
[9] Thieblot, *Davis-Bacon Act*, p. 95.
[10] Robert S. Goldfarb and John F. Morrall III, "Cost Implications of Changing Davis-Bacon Administration," *Policy Analysis*, vol. 4 (Fall 1978), pp. 439–54.
[11] Thieblot, *Davis-Bacon Act*, p. 97.

a joint effort to improve housing conditions. The 1937 Housing Act required that a substandard unit be torn down for every public housing unit built. Cleared slum land costs much more than vacant land on the fringe of cities. On the basis of land costs during the 1950s, Richard Muth concluded that housing projects built in slum areas cost over half again as much as those built elsewhere.[12] More recently, slum clearance has been less important in public housing, and the goal of the program has changed. HUD policy today is directed toward attempting to locate public housing in suburban areas rather than in central cities, often over the opposition of the localities.

The goals of promoting slum clearance and paying union wages were established by Congress. Program administrators also have goals which are similarly pursued through policies that raise costs. For example, program administrators have a strong desire to prevent scandals. The most common mechanism for this purpose is a system of regulations setting stringent procedures for both the government staff and the contractors. The effect on costs has been summarized by Irving Welfeld in the case of the Turnkey program:

> As originally conceived and operated there was little regulation of the developer. The initial experience resulted both in units far cheaper than conventionally produced and in a number of scandals. Regulations were imposed and the development process was made so much more complex that the Turnkey method is now [1972] more expensive than LHA designed and managed construction.[13]

Welfeld concludes that "rules and regulations guide the entire development process to such a degree that the overall increase in the average costs of public housing is sufficient to finance the good life for a squadron of thieves."[14]

From the administrator's standpoint the costs of scandal far exceed the benefits of reduced program cost; he or she will receive unfavorable press attention for the scandals and may receive no public credit at all for saving 10 or 20 percent per unit. The common presumption appears to be that scandal, with its illegal profits, necessarily implies higher costs for the program. The cost of preventing scandal, however, is overlooked.

Tax Exempt Bonds. The federal government pays for the construction

[12] Richard F. Muth, *Public Housing: An Economic Evaluation* (Washington, D.C.: American Enterprise Institute for Public Policy Research, 1973), p. 13.
[13] Irving H. Welfeld, *America's Housing Problem: An Approach to Its Solution* (Washington, D.C.: American Enterprise Institute for Public Policy Research, 1973), p. 18.
[14] Ibid.

of public housing projects over forty years, providing funds to local authorities so that they can pay the principal and interest on their bonds. Interest income on the bonds has been tax exempt since the public housing program was enacted in 1937; the 1981 budget, however, proposes to end this exemption.

The economic and budgetary effects of tax exemption provide an instructive case study of the logic underlying housing policy decisions. The exemption reduces direct federal budget outlays for public housing, since investors are willing to pay more for the bonds and to accept a lower rate of return. But, at the same time, this creates a large indirect cost, because the interest rate is determined by the income tax bracket of the marginal investor while investors in higher brackets receive a greater tax saving. The forgone tax revenue from the exemption is probably much greater than the increase in interest costs that the federal government would have to pay in order to float a taxable, federally guaranteed bond issue. The National Housing Policy Review estimated in 1973 that the tax exemption cost the federal government almost as much as the total direct federal and local expenditures for public housing.[15] The federal saving on a taxable bond issue would therefore be substantial.

However, taxable bonds have not been popular with housing authorities, or with federal housing officials. The increase in interest costs for taxable bonds would produce a visible federal budget expenditure and would reduce the number of units that could be subsidized out of any given budget figure. On the other hand, the indirect effect of tax exemption on overall federal revenues is much more obscure to the press and public; to the extent that it generates pressure to hold down the level of expenditures, the effect is likely to be spread among all federal programs.

Concern with budget impact rather than with overall cost is not limited to public housing or housing programs, but the difference between the two is especially great in this instance. It remains to be seen if Congress will accept the president's proposal to end the tax exemption; the narrower interests of public housing advocates are strongly in favor of the current system.

Operating Subsidies. In addition to the capital costs, the federal government now pays operating subsidies to local housing authorities to bridge the gap between operating costs and tenants' rental payments, which are limited to 25 percent of their income under the Brooke Amendment. That amendment also removes the financial

---

[15] National Housing Policy Review, *Housing in the Seventies*, 1974, p. 123.

constraint on operating expenses that had been effectively imposed by the tenants' payments, thereby necessitating some system for determining the appropriate amount of subsidy that should be budgeted by the federal government and for allocating that subsidy to individual housing authorities and projects. The mechanism used by HUD is the Performance Funding System, which estimates the operating costs for well-run projects. The system, developed by the Urban Institute as part of a long-term study of public housing,[16] is based on formulas which relate operating expenses to tenant and project characteristics in the more successful projects. The formula indicates the operating expense level that well-run projects should incur, and the operating subsidy provided by HUD is the difference between this estimated level and the project income from tenants. Nearly all projects receive some subsidy under this system, because nearly all have tenants whose incomes are insufficient to meet the operating expenses.

Overall Costs. The direct capital, indirect, and operating costs combined amount to a very hefty subsidy for public housing tenants. New units appear to cost about 25 percent more than comparable private housing, according to the most detailed economic analyses of the program.[17] The tax exemption and the Davis-Bacon Act appear to be the most important explanations of the difference. The 1981 federal budget authorizes annual payments of $5,340 for the bonds to be issued in order to finance new units. About $1,000 of this represents the difference between the tax-exempt and taxable bond interest rates and could be "saved" if tax exemption is retained; but if the 1973 analysis of the National Housing Policy Review remains valid, the tax exemption nearly doubles the annual federal cost, taking into account the forgone tax revenue. Operating subsidies currently run more than $700 million annually, or $600 per unit per year, and they are increasing steadily.

These various subsidies add up to almost $6,000 per year, or

---

[16] Robert Sadacca, Morton Isler, and Joan DeWitt, *The Development of a Prototype Equation for Public Housing Operating Expenses* (Washington, D.C.: The Urban Institute, 1976).

[17] See Eugene Smolensky, "Public Housing or Income Supplements: The Economics of Housing for the Poor," *Journal of the American Institute of Planners*, vol. 34 (March 1968), pp. 94–101; David M. Barton and Edgar O. Olsen, "The Benefits and Costs of Public Housing in New York City" (Madison: University of Wisconsin Institute for Research on Poverty, 1976); Frank de Leeuw and Sam H. Leaman, "The Section 23 Leasing Program," in U.S. Congress, Joint Economic Committee, *The Economics of Federal Subsidy Programs*, part 5: *Housing Subsidies*, 92nd Cong., 2nd sess., October 1972, pp. 642–59.

slightly under $500 per month, for each unit.[18] If that amount were provided directly to public housing tenants, it would enable them to rent almost any new apartment now being built privately. The subsidy by itself is nearly as much as the most recent poverty-level income ($6,662 for a family of four in 1978), though again the data should be adjusted to take account of inflation in order to be comparable.[19] If the subsidy were given in cash directly to the tenants, it would be enough to lift virtually all of them out of poverty.

Subsidies of this magnitude are politically possible only because they are provided for a small fraction of the eligible population. One of the most serious criticisms of public housing has been that it is fundamentally inequitable: a large benefit goes to a few households while nothing goes to a very large number that are similarly situated. For example, in 1972 some 850,000 households with incomes under $5,000, out of 17.7 million in that income range, were living in public housing. Roughly speaking, one family in twenty was being subsidized. The problem arises in virtually every housing program but is most pronounced in construction programs, because the subsidy is so large.

Older public housing projects incur substantially lower direct and indirect costs because they were built when interest rates were lower. However, older projects receive further subsidy from the federal government. Since 1967 HUD has provided funds for the modernization of older projects because they are deteriorating or becoming obsolescent. These improvements are financed by the local authorities in the same manner as the initial construction, through bonds: the federal government provides the funds to repay principal and interest over a twenty-year amortization period. Currently, the government is financing over $500 million worth of modernization

---

[18] Similar calculations have recently been made by the Congressional Budget Office (CBO). This study finds that the annual debt-service cost will be about $3,200 per unit, slightly above the figure used in the text. The CBO's estimate of the cost of the tax exemption, however, is substantially lower, ranging from $42,600 to $64,200, or about $1,000 to $1,500 per year, depending on the rate of inflation. Offsetting this, CBO estimates that operating subsidies will increase and will cost between $2,400 and $7,400 per unit annually over forty years, again depending on the rate of inflation. Thus, the CBO estimate of the capital cost (including tax exemption) is about $4,300 to $4,900 per year, less than the $5,340 budget estimate, while the total cost ranges from $6,700 to $12,300, far more than the author's figure of $6,000. The CBO's attempt to estimate the rate of inflation is the main reason for the difference. Whichever set of calculations proves more nearly correct, it is clear that public housing is a very expensive program. U.S. Congressional Budget Office, *Long-Term Costs of Housing Programs*, pp. 36–37.
[19] U.S. Bureau of the Census, *Money Income and Poverty Status of Families and Persons in the United States: 1978 (Advance Report)*, series P–60, no. 120, 1979, p. 36.

annually, budgeting about $1 billion to pay for each year's improvements.

Modernization is limited to major repairs and other improvements that may legitimately be capitalized. Much of the work presently being carried out is necessitated by relatively recent changes in federal, state, or local laws; such work includes "retrofitting" projects to make them accessible to the handicapped and removing lead-based paint from interior walls.

Energy conservation is also receiving priority in line with general federal policy and the special problems of public housing. Utility increases have been a major factor in rising operating costs. Most projects have not had meters for individual units, and modernization funds are being used to install them. Meters by themselves will not encourage conservation, since tenants can still be charged only 25 percent of their income for operating expenses (including utilities), but meters will permit project managers to determine which tenants are using more electricity and heating fuel and perhaps to put informal pressure on those tenants to reduce consumption.

Problems Confronting Projects. Public housing projects face serious problems in addition to financial difficulties. Many have acquired reputations of being worse living environments than the slums they were supposed to replace. The program's advocates and administrators recognize the existence, in some projects, of social problems ranging from inadequate tenant maintenance to vandalism to high crime rates.[20] A variety of prescriptions have been offered to deal with these problems and improve the quality of life in the projects.

Management problems. Many of the problems have been blamed on poor project management on the part of the local housing authorities. Research conducted by the Urban Institute for HUD has identified several management characteristics that appear both to increase tenant satisfaction with the projects and to lower operating expenses.[21] Foremost among these is firmness: successful projects tend to enforce their rules strictly, including the rules on tenant behavior. Strict enforcement apparently does not create tenant resentment; on the contrary, tenants are more satisfied with their treatment than in less stringently managed projects.

---

[20] National Commission on Urban Problems, *Building the American City* (New York: Praeger, 1969), p. 123.
[21] Robert Sadacca et al., *Management Performance in Public Housing* (Washington, D.C.: The Urban Institute, 1974), pp. 44–60.

Perhaps equally important is the management's responsiveness to tenant problems and concerns. In successful projects tenants know who to contact for repairs, and management responds quickly. Major and minor repairs are done properly, with few instances of poor workmanship. Prompt repairs are made more easily when individual project managers have greater day-to-day power to run the projects and when fewer decisions need to be referred to the local housing authority's central office.

Management procedures in many authorities have failed to provide information about what is actually occurring in projects,[22] and maintenance has been one major problem area. Most authorities have until recently lacked adequate maintenance and inventory information systems to keep track of what work is being done, how rapidly, and at what cost. Many authorities still lack up-to-date information systems. Tenant account records frequently consist of a box of index cards in the project manager's office.

Modern accounting and management systems cost money to set up, although they should result in savings in the long run. Most local authorities have little to spend on such systems. HUD has funded several programs to enable the authorities to update management techniques. The programs appear to work in the sense that the financial performance of management improves and tenant satisfaction increases, but the need for separate management improvement programs points out the weakness of local housing authorities as project managers. Private landlords and property managers finance improvements in their procedures from the income from their property, not from government subsidies.

Improved management can undoubtedly increase the well-being of project residents and should be sought for that reason alone. But even an extremely well-run project is a very expensive way to house the poor; management can do little about the inherent costliness of subsidized new construction. Operating subsidies account for only about 10 percent of the total direct and indirect federal expenditure on public housing, and it is unlikely that any degree of improvement could enable public housing authorities to run their projects without any operating subsidies at all; no matter how improved the management, public housing would therefore still cost at least 90 percent as much as at present.

In recent years the concept of tenant management as a means of improving the living environment of projects has gained popularity

---

[22] David Carlson, *Public Housing in Transition: 25 Case Studies* (Washington, D.C.: The Urban Institute, 1977), pp. 22–25.

in public housing.[23] Under such arrangements, tenant organizations are given responsibility for day-to-day project operations.

Several projects are now experimenting with tenant management, and their experience is being analyzed. Preliminary findings indicate, however, that there has been relatively little improvement, at least from the standpoint of the tenants. Project managers and public housing authority staff believe that project conditions have improved, but tenants in tenant management projects are generally only slightly more satisfied than those in other projects, and the differences are seldom statistically significant.[24] Further analysis may modify these findings, but it seems likely that improvements will be small at best. Most tenants lack management skills or experience, but they are probably more concerned than anyone else is about the project they live in. Property management requires more than interest and concern, however—although it certainly requires them—and the skills needed are seldom acquired quickly.

Locational problems. Frequently, the social problems of public housing are blamed on the physical or locational characteristics of the projects. The Douglas Commission in 1968 asserted that problem projects were, typically, large high rises in big cities. The commission argued that smaller buildings, scattered through a municipality or metropolitan area, would alleviate the anonymity and feeling of powerlessness in people that brought about antisocial behavior.[25]

The Urban Institute's study of projects reached conclusions that are, in part, similar. The more successful projects tended to have lower densities; however, high-rise projects per se were not significantly worse than low-rise projects. The study also found that crime and vandalism were more serious problems in large metropolitan areas, but it did not distinguish between city and suburban locations. The study did find, however, that less successful projects were located in less desirable neighborhoods which were regarded as continuing to deteriorate.[26]

Spatial deconcentration of the very poor would probably improve the quality of their housing—and certainly of their environment. Unfortunately, deconcentration has proved difficult to accomplish in the public housing program. Suburban jurisdictions are generally

---

[23] Martin Mayer, *The Builders* (New York: W. W. Norton and Co., 1978), pp. 196–205.
[24] Suzanne B. Loux and Robert Sadacca, *A Preliminary Analysis of the Tenant Management Demonstration Program* (Washington, D.C.: The Urban Institute, 1980).
[25] National Commission on Urban Problems, *Building the American City*, p. 127.
[26] Sadacca et al., *Management Performance in Public Housing*, pp. 25–33.

unwilling to permit projects other than those for the elderly. Many city neighborhoods have taken the same stance. For many years the Chicago Housing Authority would not build a project in any ward in which the alderman opposed it. This practice was finally enjoined by a federal court, which required future projects to be dispersed through the city and through the metropolitan area as well. Since then no projects have been built in Chicago. A number of cases in other areas have been working their way through the courts, but little public or subsidized housing has been built in the suburbs.

Deconcentration or economic integration is more likely to be achieved where it is unobtrusive. A new apartment project constructed specifically for the poor is not unobtrusive, whether it is low rise or high rise. On the contrary, it focuses neighborhood attention on the new residents. The project is likely to generate hostility rather than achieve integration. Deconcentration is more likely to occur when low-income families are subsidized to live in existing housing, because their presence is less generally noticeable. Even if these families are different from their neighbors racially, for example, their housing is not different from their neighbors' housing. Deconcentration is difficult to achieve by government action in any case, but the Section 8 existing housing program is probably more successful in this respect than is conventional public housing.

Tenant characteristics. The problems of public housing are also often blamed on the changing nature of the tenants. Since the advent of the Brooke Amendment and the court decisions limiting the ability of local authorities to select tenants, residents' incomes have declined and there is an increasing preponderance of families on welfare or headed by females. Experienced public housing officials and managers have frequently argued that projects were more attractive places to live and were easier to manage before these changes took place. Their views are sometimes echoed by longtime tenants.[27] Complaints about public housing, however, long antedate the Brooke Amendment, and the Urban Institute study finds relatively little evidence to support this contention.[28] Less successful projects—those providing less satisfaction to tenants and incurring higher operating expenses—do have more households on welfare than do other projects, but, apart from this, tenant characteristics are unrelated to project quality when other characteristics of the project (such as neighbor-

---

[27] An especially vigorous presentation of this argument is contained in Mayer, *The Builders.*

[28] Sadacca et al., *Management Performance in Public Housing,* pp. 31–32.

hood conditions) are taken into account. This analysis is not conclusive, since the characteristics of the tenants may influence the characteristics of the neighborhood, but even ignoring the neighborhood, few attributes of tenants have been found to be related to project performance or tenant satisfaction. Attributes which have been found *not* related include household size, single-parent households, teenage school dropouts, adult unemployment, personal problems, health problems, inability to speak English, and education level.

While this research indicates that tenant characteristics are not responsible for the problems of public housing, the fact that the issue is raised at all is an ironic commentary on the change in perception about public housing. When the program was established in the 1930s, improved housing was expected to ameliorate social problems. Now program officials, tenants, and some analysts are willing to believe that social problems are affecting housing conditions (and for the worse), instead of the other way around.

Section 8 New Construction

Program Characteristics. The Section 8 subsidy program for newly constructed dwellings operates in much the same way as conventional public housing. The subsidy is given to a particular project and not to an individual household. As in public housing, HUD makes a commitment to subsidize tenants before the project is built. The amount of subsidy depends on the income of the individual; this does not differ from public housing since the Brooke Amendment or the rent supplement program. Tenant selection is made by the owner of the project, not by HUD.

There are differences in the operation of the programs. Perhaps the most important is that, in Section 8 new construction, the decision whether to build Section 8 units or to subsidize existing housing is based on a locality's assessment of its own housing market. This assessment is contained in the Housing Assistance Plan (HAP) drawn up by the locality, as required under the 1974 Housing and Community Development Act (the legislation creating Section 8).[29] The total amount of assistance provided in the federal budget for Section 8 is supposed to be allocated in accordance with the HAPs so that the mix of new, existing, and substantially rehabilitated housing reflects local priorities.

There has been continuing controversy over the role of the HAPs in determining the Section 8 mix. The municipality or county incurs

---

[29] P. L. 93–383, Sec. 213.

no cost if it chooses new or rehabilitated housing, even though costs per unit are much higher for these programs. The locality need only look at the benefits to its citizens. If the new housing is better than that currently available, then low-income families will benefit more, at no cost to the locality, if it asks for new housing. Furthermore, construction of the new housing will stimulate the local economy. At first, HUD sought to counter the incentives for new construction by developing standards for assessing local housing market conditions and evaluating the "need" for subsidized new housing. In 1976, however, Congress required that the HAPs be taken into account by HUD to the maximum possible extent. This created difficulties in program administration at the federal level, because the total number of subsidized units cannot be known accurately for budget or planning purposes and is subject to continual change as HAPs are modified. On the other hand, the localities frequently complain that HUD attempts to dictate or influence the contents of the plan. A critical review of the HAP formulation process by Raymond Struyk, formerly a deputy assistant secretary at HUD, supported this contention. Struyk found that HUD had urged localities to stress existing housing under the Republican administration in 1975 and 1976, and to stress housing construction under the Democrats in the next three years. The net effect of HUD pressure, limited local data, and other factors is that "the HAPs were essentially random with respect to market conditions."[30] No planning requirement analogous to the HAP exists for public housing.

Section 8 is open to private developers and nonprofit sponsors as well as to public housing agencies, so that a wider range of entities may respond to a HUD invitation to bid on designing and building a new project. Except under Turnkey, public housing projects have been designed by local authorities only. These differences, however, do not affect the basic similarity between the programs, particularly in regard to the "supply-side" nature of the subsidy: housing units rather than households are subsidized in the first instance. A tenant who moves out of either public housing or Section 8 new construction loses the subsidy; the new tenant in the unit receives it in his or her stead.

At the end of fiscal year 1977, 165,000 Section 8 units had been built, and another 227,000 were under construction.[31] A further

[30] Raymond J. Struyk, *Saving the Housing Assistance Plan* (Washington, D.C.: The Urban Institute, 1979), pp. 14–15.
[31] The HUD budget does not identify the number of new Section 8 units actually occupied, but it appears that at least three-quarters of those completed at the end of 1979 were also occupied; the actual fraction is probably higher, since over 90 percent of all completed Section 8 units (new, existing, and rehabilitated) were also occupied.

153,000 were in the HUD processing pipeline, but construction had not begun and subsidy contracts had not been executed. HUD hopes to approve 90,000 units in fiscal year 1980 and 115,000 in 1981.

There appears to be about a year's lag between HUD approval and the start of construction, and another eighteen months to completion. The latter is not a particularly long period, but the rate of construction was slower than had occurred with Section 236, particularly in the first few years, and the program came under substantial political criticism for this reason. The criticism was intensified because the enactment of the program coincided with a sharp downturn in housing production which was particularly severe in apartment building, and both builders and members of Congress wanted the program to mitigate the housing cycle. Dissatisfaction with the production rate caused Congress to reactivate the conventional public housing program in 1976.

As with public housing, part of the explanation for the longer production process in Section 8 lies in the increasing insistence that housing programs serve "social goals" as well as producing housing. Section 8 projects are subject to the same review processes as public housing. In addition, projects may be insured by the Federal Housing Administration (FHA); in such cases, a parallel FHA processing cycle is necessary, which takes additional time. The same is true of projects insured by the Farmers Home Administration.

Families living in new Section 8 projects typically have somewhat higher incomes than those in public housing or Section 8 existing housing: the median family income in 1977 was about $4,300, some 20 percent above that in the other two programs.[32] Over 40 percent were elderly, and over 40 percent consisted of one person; undoubtedly almost all of these were elderly. Only 6 percent consisted of more than four persons. The other programs had fewer elderly or single persons, and more large families. The concentration of elderly and single persons in Section 8 new construction indicates that the income difference for families of the same type is greater than the median income figures suggest, since elderly and single persons generally have lower incomes than younger individuals and families, even among the poor. Only about one-sixth received any welfare income, but undoubtedly more received Social Security and other retirement income. Data on the proportion employed are not available.

It is probable that the program will serve the elderly still more extensively as it progresses. A 1977 HUD survey found that almost

---

[32] U.S. Congressional Budget Office, *Federal Housing Policy: Current Programs and Recurring Issues*, June 1978, p. 28.

two-thirds of the units were intended for the elderly. The high proportion of projects for the elderly reflects the HAPs prepared by local governments, but it far exceeds the incidence of elderly in the eligible population.

Section 8 can be used in combination with the Section 202 program for the elderly. Section 202 has been a small program (some 45,000 units were built from 1959 to 1972), which provided loans from the U.S. Treasury to nonprofit sponsors of housing for the elderly. The Treasury loans carry a lower interest rate than do conventional or FHA-insured mortgages; the interest rate has varied, ranging from a flat 3 percent to the Treasury's long-term borrowing rate. At present the rate is based on the average Treasury rate during the preceding fiscal year. This is not low enough to enable the low-income elderly, or even elderly persons with average incomes, to live in Section 202 projects without additional subsidy; therefore, HUD has combined the two programs, providing Section 8 subsidies for all Section 202 projects. Section 202 has taken priority over other Section 8 projects: in some areas little or no money is available for anything else.

Section 8 is intended to encourage economic integration within projects, but in practice virtually all proposed new projects have planned to subsidize all tenants. This may result in part from HUD's own rules, which require project developers to state the maximum percentage of subsidized units that they expect within the project. This percentage cannot subsequently be raised should the developer's expectations change, so that the prudent course of action is to ask for 100 percent subsidy.[33]

Program Costs. The cost of new Section 8 apartments is high. The subsidy per household in 1977 was $2,460 annually or $205 per month.[34] This is approximately double the subsidy in the existing housing program, even though the latter serves households with lower incomes. Projected costs for the future are substantially higher. The federal budget for fiscal 1981 estimates the budget outlay at $5,300 to $5,450 per year, or about $450 per month, over the thirty-year life of the subsidy. For several reasons, this figure is not a reliable guide to actual outlays. As is customary with budget cost projections, it is based on the assumption that the tenant pays no rent, which implies that he or she has no income. This is rarely the case. This is more

[33] Grace Milgram, *The Current State of the Section 8 Housing Programs* (Washington, D.C.: Library of Congress, Congressional Research Service, 1977), p. 25.
[34] U.S. Office of Management and Budget, *The Budget of the United States Government, Fiscal Year 1980*, 1979, p. 261.

than offset, however, because the projection apparently ignores inflation, assuming that costs will be constant over the next thirty years. Calculations based on modest (by current standards) inflation rates in the range of 3 to 7 percent for both fair market rents (FMRs) and tenant incomes yield lifetime expected budget outlays of $5,400 to $11,400 per year.[35] Special tax benefits and other indirect subsidies add another $400 to $600. The larger figure, while extremely high by today's standards, should not be given too much emphasis, since it represents the cumulating effect of inflation much more than the cost of the program in current dollars. It does suggest the possible long-term impact of commitments now being made by the federal government, however. In today's dollars the annual cost is projected to range from $2,700 to $3,000. The difference between these figures and the $5,300 or more projected in the budget is primarily due to the fact that CBO attempts to project the income and rent contributions of the assisted tenants, to arrive at a net cost to the government.

The inflationless outlay of $450 per month is about 50 percent more than the monthly rental on new apartments now being offered in the private market, according to Census Bureau data.[36] This comparison probably understates the true cost difference, since a higher percentage of Section 8 apartments are efficiencies and one-bedroom units.[37] At least some of the difference is due to the additional paperwork required by the government, which raises costs as well as lengthening the processing time. Part is also undoubtedly due to the Davis-Bacon Act requirement that workers be paid "prevailing" wages, which applies to Section 8 construction as well as public housing.

The high cost of Section 8 has been used as an argument for public housing. In 1976 the Congressional Research Service of the Library of Congress estimated that overall costs for the older program were lower by about $120 per unit annually.[38] This occasioned a political controversy at the time. HUD developed comparable calculations indicating that the overall difference was in favor of Section

---

[35] Congressional Budget Office, *Long-Term Costs of Housing Programs*, pp. 21–25.

[36] U.S. Bureau of the Census, *Market Absorptions of Apartments, Annual: 1979 Absorptions*, Current Housing Reports, series H–130–79–5, 1980.

[37] Gilmer Blankespoor and Susan Jaffee, "The New Construction Program," in U.S. Department of Housing and Urban Development, Office of Policy Development and Research, *Lower Income Housing Assistance Program (Section 8): Interim Findings of Evaluation of Research*, February 1978, p. 162.

[38] Morton J. Schussheim, *Comparative Costs and Estimated Households Eligible for Participation in Certain Federally Assisted Low Income Housing Programs*, a report prepared for the U.S. Congress, Senate, Committee on Banking, Housing, and Urban Affairs, 1976, p. 4.

8 by about $25.[39] These cost calculations are complex and to some extent the differences reflect differences in assumptions which can only be proved right or wrong when the program is in operation. The differences are small in budget terms; even $120 per unit over a thirty-year period for 200,000 units (more new construction than has been proposed in any budget since 1974) becomes $900 million—a tidy sum, but less than 4 percent of one year's budget authority for housing. But the overall costs of both programs are large, especially in comparison with the cost of Section 8 existing housing. The Library of Congress estimated overall costs of over $3,500 per unit per year for each program, and HUD's estimates were around $3,800.[40] Regardless of which program turns out to be slightly less expensive, both are very costly ways of providing better housing to the poor.

The high construction and debt service costs imply that fair market rents must be high, so that the subsidy and the tenant's payment enable the project owner to meet the debt service on the mortgage. Fair market rents for new units are substantially higher than for existing apartments, even though both are supposed to be measures of the cost of modest decent housing in the private market. New units do not necessarily rent for the new unit FMR, however. Rents are also subject to a "rent reasonableness" test; they must be in the same range as those on recently constructed unsubsidized apartment projects of modest design. A HUD appraiser makes the comparison, using three to five projects to determine the comparable rent. Thus, new Section 8 projects must meet two rent tests, both of which purport to measure the same thing.

Project developers have objected to the rent reasonableness tests, arguing that their costs are higher because of Davis-Bacon and HUD construction standards, and also that their management costs will be higher. Many have urged that the rents be based on construction costs rather than on market rents. The same argument has been advanced by many HUD area office staff.[41] If this approach were adopted, the program would be freed from the discipline of the market: builders would have no incentive to hold down costs, and the

---

[39] U.S. Congress, Senate, Committee on Banking, Housing, and Urban Affairs, *Oversight on Department of Housing and Urban Development*, 94th Cong., 2nd sess., June 23, 1976, pp. 26–31.

[40] As has been explained in the previous section of this chapter, direct costs are lower in public housing because the local housing authority's bonds are tax exempt. The forgone federal income taxes on the bonds approximately offset the direct cost advantage in the Library of Congress and HUD calculations.

[41] Blankespoor and Jaffee, "The New Construction Program," p. 174.

only pressure on expenditures would come from the HUD budget, where the total available subsidy is fixed. The procedure would be much like that employed for the mortgage subsidy program in the early 1970s and would have the same potential for scandal.

To date, HUD has refused to base fair market rents directly on construction costs; however, it has adopted a rent adjustment system which may have the same effect. Projects can charge higher rents if they fall in any of several categories: 10 percent more for projects housing the elderly or handicapped (because of the need for special design features), 10 percent more for projects in which all tenants are subsidized (because of higher management costs), and 5 percent more for *both* FHA-insured and conventionally financed projects. The adjustment for insured projects is because of discount points on the mortgage, necessitated by the below-market FHA ceiling rate, while the conventionally financed project limits are raised because of higher conventional interest rates. The discount points, however, serve to raise the effective rate on FHA-insured mortgages to the market rate, so the net effect is that both types of projects get the further subsidy simply because interest rates are high, even though the comparable private projects must pay the same rates. Nearly all projects qualify for at least one adjustment. The HUD area office can also permit a further 5 percent increase because of unique market conditions such as high construction costs. These adjustments are cumulative, so that a 100 percent subsidized FHA-insured (or conventional) project for the elderly in a high-cost area can charge rents that are 33 percent above the FMR. With these adjustments and with changes in FMRs, project developers' concerns over FMRs appear to be diminishing.

A further device is available for holding down mortgage interest costs and, thus, the needed rents. Section 8 projects are eligible for below-market interest rates through the Tandem Plan, described in chapter 3. The Government National Mortgage Association (GNMA) makes commitments to buy mortgages with below-market rates at par so that private lenders can issue the mortgages knowing that they can sell them to GNMA. That agency in turn resells them, through an auction, at whatever price they can bring on the open market. Since the market interest rate is above the contract rate, the mortgages sell at a discount which is absorbed by the federal government; roughly speaking, the discount is proportional to the difference between market and contract interest rates.

Through this procedure the project developer need pay only 7.5 percent interest on the mortgage instead of 10 percent (in recent years), and thus needs to charge only four-fifths as much for debt service as part of the rent. The overall subsidy cost to the government is about the same, regardless of whether the Tandem Plan is used, but the subsidy attributed to Section 8 in the federal budget is smaller when it is used.

State HFAs. State Housing Finance Agencies (HFAs) also participate in Section 8, but in so different a way from private developers and local housing authorities that they deserve separate discussion. State HFAs have become important participants in subsidized housing in the last fifteen years. Before 1965 only New York had such an agency; by 1973 there were thirty, and in 1978 there were thirty-seven active agencies. They were extensively involved in producing housing under the Section 236 program and have been expected to finance a significant amount of new Section 8 construction. As one aspect of the New Federalism of the Nixon administration, subsidized housing production was to devolve to states and localities as much as possible.[42]

State HFAs have the same advantage of tax exemption for their bonds that local housing authorities have. For this reason, they were originally expected to build subsidized housing more cheaply than private developers and thus to charge lower rents and require less subsidy, by about $500 per unit annually.[43] However, the direct cost advantage may have disappeared; the last two budgets project the per-year subsidy to be almost exactly the same for state HFA projects as for those financed in other ways.[44] If this is correct, the total cost for the state projects will be higher, because of their tax exemption, which probably adds about $1,000 annually in indirect costs.[45]

HUD treats the state agencies differently from private developers and local housing authorities. Their proposals are processed under a special "fast track" system, which allows them to conduct their own rent reasonableness tests. As a Library of Congress study of the program has noted, "They tend to a sufficient liberality of interpretation to make their projects feasible."[46] In addition, their mortgages can be amortized over a forty-year period because they are guaranteed the subsidy by HUD for that period; private projects are guaranteed for

---

[42] A discussion of state Housing Finance Agencies is contained in National Housing Policy Review, *Housing in the Seventies*, chap. 5.

[43] Schussheim, *Comparative Costs and Estimated Households*, p. 4; Senate Banking Committee, *Oversight on HUD*, pp. 32–36.

[44] Office of Management and Budget, *U.S. 1980 Budget*, p. 261; Department of Housing and Urban Development, *1981 HUD Budget Summary*, p. H–9.

[45] Schussheim, *Comparative Costs and Estimated Households*, p. 4; Senate Banking Committee, *Oversight on HUD*, pp. 32–36.

[46] Milgram, *Current State of Section 8*, p. 43.

only thirty years.[47] This permits lower debt amortization charges each year.

Even as Section 8 was being enacted, state HFAs were having some difficulty in marketing their bonds. The next year saw the New York City fiscal crisis—touched off by the inability of the city's HFA to float bonds on some housing projects—and the marketability of many state HFA bond issues dropped sharply. This occurred at the same time as the cyclical decline in unsubsidized apartment construction, which created political pressure to assist the agencies.

The HFAs have sought three forms of help from the federal government: subsidies for taxable bonds, a federal guarantee of their tax exempt bonds, and coinsurance of their projects. Funds for the taxable bond subsidies were appropriated by Congress in 1975, but the bond market improved before the program was implemented and no state applied for the funds. In 1979 the Carter administration persuaded Congress to rescind the appropriation, and the funds are no longer available.

A coinsurance program was announced by HUD in 1976, but was criticized by the state agencies as not being sufficiently generous with respect to the division of the risk between the agencies and HUD. In 1979, responding to the criticism, HUD revised the plan. To date, there is no experience by which to evaluate this program; although several states have received approval from HUD, none has yet issued bonds to finance coinsured project mortgages.[48]

The federal guarantee would place the state agencies on the same basis as the local housing authorities. This would be an ironic ending to this chapter of the New Federalism; the state agencies would receive their subsidies from the federal government and would be protected by the federal government from the consequences of their mistakes.

Section 8 Substantial Rehabilitation

A companion program to Section 8 new construction provides subsidies in the same way for existing apartments requiring extensive

---

[47] Like the state HFAs, private developers are expected to take out forty-year mortgages but are guaranteed subsidy for only thirty years (originally twenty years). Since most of the principal would remain outstanding at the end of thirty years, the private developers have to charge rents high enough to amortize the mortgage in that period, obtain a further subsidy through Section 8 or another program, or rent to tenants who can pay market rents. The gap between length of subsidy and length of mortgage has been a recurring complaint of the developers.

[48] "Tax-exempt Bonds, Coinsurance Vital to State Agencies, CSHA Official Says," *Housing and Development Reporter*, December 20, 1979, p. 610.

rehabilitation (usually defined as more than 25 percent of the total value of the rehabilitated structure). The purpose of the program is much the same as that of new construction—to encourage housing production and ensure that the poor live in better housing than they would occupy without the subsidy. The program may also help to revitalize city neighborhoods.

To date, this program has been small, though it is growing. At the end of fiscal year 1979, about 21,000 rehabilitated units had been completed, about 60,000 started, and about 104,000 approved by HUD.

About half of those started and 40 percent of those approved were for the elderly or handicapped. Approvals are projected to increase to 25,000 in both fiscal 1980 and 1981, but this should be regarded as problematical: federal rehabilitation programs since the days of urban renewal have consistently and substantially overestimated their prospective activity. Optimism is endemic to HUD program administrators in their budget projections, but rarely to the same extent in programs consisting of either new production or existing housing. The budget for fiscal 1979 anticipated 70,000 approved units; the budget for fiscal 1980 estimated 52,000 approved units in fiscal 1979; actual approvals were 33,000.

The program is too small to be evaluated systematically, but it is clearly expensive. The 1981 HUD budget estimated that annual subsidies per unit would range from $5,700 to $6,300, depending on the type of sponsor; this is more than the costs for Section 8 new construction.

Section 8 Existing Housing

Despite the fact that they were created at the same time and share the same section of the housing legislation, Section 8 "new construction" and "existing housing" are in reality quite distinct programs. They are administered separately by HUD, offer subsidy through different mechanisms, and are operated differently on the local level. They also have rather different bases of political support.

Program Characteristics. Section 8 existing housing is designed to rely primarily on the efforts of individual low-income households to provide themselves with better housing. A household first applies for Section 8 assistance from the local agency administering the program (usually a local public housing authority). If it qualifies, the household is given a certificate promising that it will receive a rent subsidy to enable it to live in an acceptable housing unit—one which meets the local authority's quality standards and which rents for no more than the fair market rent established by HUD. Typically, the household has sixty days in which to find such a unit, after which the certificate lapses and is offered to another household. If the household finds an acceptable unit, it receives a subsidy amounting to the difference between the rent of the unit and 25 percent of the household's income (15 percent for very poor large families and those with heavy medical expenses).

As of September 1979 almost 550,000 households were receiving assistance through the Section 8 program. An additional 120,000 are projected through fiscal 1981.

Income limits for eligibility vary with the size of the family, ranging from 50 percent of the area's median income for a single person to the actual median for a family of eight or more. The figure is 80 percent of the median for a family of four, which is commonly referred to as "the" income limit. Until 1978 single persons who were not elderly were excluded. There is a further requirement that at least 30 percent of the households assisted in each jurisdiction must have incomes below 50 percent of the local median. This requirement has not proved to be a constraint, however. Over 80 percent of subsidy recipients fall into this very low income category; the median income of assisted households is around $3,500. This is closely comparable to the income of public housing tenants—although Section 8 is, in fact, open to households with much higher incomes.

There are several possible explanations for the underrepresentation of the relatively well-to-do among subsidy recipients. They may be choosing not to participate, or they may not be selected by local authorities to receive certificates, or they may be unsuccessful in locating housing that is acceptable both to themselves and to the local authority. There is some evidence in support of the last explanation: unsuccessful participants in the program (those who have received certificates but have failed to find acceptable housing) had incomes about $1,000 higher on average than subsidy recipients.[49] Families including at least one wage earner have been similarly disproportionately unsuccessful.

A common criticism of Section 8 is that it is inadequate in serving large families because private landlords are unwilling to rent to such

---

[49] Unless otherwise indicated, information on the Section 8 existing program is taken from Margaret Drury et al., *Lower Income Housing Assistance Program (Section 8)* (Washington, D.C.: The Urban Institute, 1978).

families.[50] The perceived shortage of larger units on the private market is offered as justification for a greater emphasis on new construction of public housing. This argument is less than convincing. Large families, like small ones, are already living in private housing: some landlords must be willing to rent to them. The record of public housing in serving large families has also been criticized; ten years ago the Douglas Commission complained that there were not enough large units being built.[51] The complaint is perennial in housing programs; moreover, in the case of Section 8 the underrepresentation is more apparent than real.

It is true that large families are less successful than smaller ones in finding satisfactory apartments, but large families generally have higher incomes and are thus more frequently found in the higher brackets of the eligible population than in the very low-income group primarily participating in the program. Data from the Annual Housing Survey suggest that large families comprise less than 10 percent of those with very low incomes; this implies that they are being assisted proportionately by the program, as 11 percent of the recipients are large families.

More than half of the units being rented through the program are single-family houses, even though such homes comprise only one-third of all rental units, and about one-quarter of the lower priced ones. This distinguishes Section 8 existing housing from other government subsidy programs, which rarely provide a chance to rent houses. The second most common type of housing is the small apartment building, with two to six units. Like the properties, the landlords are typically "small." More than half own fewer than ten units; more than a third, only one. For them, owning rental property is likely to be a part-time business. Most manage their own property, instead of hiring others. These small landlords participate heavily in the program, renting more than half their units to subsidy recipients. Generally speaking, they had low vacancy rates in their properties, and low turnover, before participating.

Section 8 permits subsidy payments to households that wish to stay in their present housing provided it meets the program standards. About half the subsidy recipients are in-place tenants. They are disproportionately elderly, most of whom live alone. These tenants

---

[50] U.S. Department of Housing and Urban Development, Office of Program Analysis and Evaluation, *Section 8 Housing Assistance Payments Program: Existing Housing—A Field Study,* 1976, pp. 7–8; Anne M. Smith et al., *Descriptions and Evaluations of Selected Housing Subsidy Programs* (Washington, D.C.: Library of Congress, Congressional Research Service, 1978), p. 16.

[51] National Commission on Urban Problems, *Building the American City,* p. 127.

are able to continue living where they want to, at a reduction in their rent burden. Apparently the program is enabling many of these elderly persons to avoid having to move.[52] Those remaining in place have frequently benefited from better housing as well: one-third of the units they occupy failed the initial quality inspection and were subsequently repaired. Average expenditures for repair have run between $275 and $300, most commonly for electrical repairs, storm window installation, painting, plastering, and repairs to outside stairs.

Most of those who have moved in order to participate in Section 8 have improved their housing markedly. One-third have moved into larger units, and three-quarters feel that they have moved into better housing. Most have also moved into a different neighborhood, and the majority think the new neighborhood is better than the old. Minorities appear to be particularly satisfied in this respect. There appears to be no effect to date on the extent of racial integration. Although both blacks and whites tend to move to neighborhoods with a higher percentage of whites, the rate of movement is about the same for subsidy recipients and unsubsidized households of each race.

Rents. The fair market rents for existing housing were originally set at the median rent in each metropolitan area for standard quality housing units of a given size, on the basis of 1970 census data adjusted for price changes. Current FMRs, however, are substantially higher than this. There are numerous exceptions to the published FMR schedule, all of which effectively raise the allowable rents. A local authority has the right to approve rents that are 10 percent above the FMRs for 20 percent of the subsidized units within its jurisdiction, and it can request the same exception from HUD for more units. Most requests for exceptions have been granted.[53]

FMRs are supposed to be uniform throughout an entire metropolitan area, but another exception has been available which effectively undermines this uniformity. HUD may approve a local request for maximum rents·that are 20 percent above the FMR for all units of a given size or type. Approval of this increase is virtually automatic for a locality in which median rents are higher than the standard metropolitan statistical area (SMSA) median. The justification for this

---

[52] Department of Housing and Urban Development, Office of Program Analysis and Evaluation, *Section 8: Existing Housing,* p. 23.

[53] Department of Housing and Urban Development, Office of Policy Development and Research, *Lower Income Housing Assistance Program,* pp.134–36.

exception is that higher rents are required because a small fraction of the units in these localities rent for less than the published FMR. The subsidies are allocated by HUD to local housing authorities, which commonly have jurisdictions smaller than an entire SMSA. Suburban housing authorities are thought to be unable to provide assistance to local residents because rents are higher than the area-wide FMRs; however, available evidence casts doubt on this argument. A fairly large fraction of the units in affluent suburban counties do in fact rent for less than the SMSA median. For example, in both Westchester County, New York, and Fairfax County, Virginia, more than a quarter of all units rented for less than the SMSA median in 1970. Also, as rents are typically high where incomes are high and vice versa, a smaller share of the population in these jurisdictions is likely to be eligible for Section 8. This exception adds to program costs without solving a clearly defined problem.

Still another, higher, exception is available for units built within the past six years. These "recently completed" units may be subsidized at rents that are up to 75 percent of the new construction FMR. Since FMRs on existing units are approximately half those on new ones, the recently completed FMR roughly splits the difference. The justification appears to be that these apartments are better than older units and therefore are worth more. This may be true, but such exceptions are not consistent with the purpose of the program, which is to enable low-income families to live in decent housing of modest quality. The FMR is supposed to serve as a limit on the quality of the housing that the government will assist low-income families to live in.

In addition to these various exceptions to the FMR schedule, local authorities can appeal for increases to the entire schedule on the grounds that the published FMRs are generally too low.

The net effect of these changes is that the fair market rents—the "official" government estimates of the cost of a decent home—are above the actual rents of half or more of the rental housing stock in each metropolitan area. The FMRs for recently completed units are above the actual rents of almost three-quarters of the existing stock of apartments.

The local authorities have an obvious incentive to seek higher FMRs. Their administrative fee is set at 8.5 percent of the FMR, so that their income increases when the FMR does. In addition to this, the program is easier to administer if the FMR is higher, since more units are available at the higher rent and certificate holders are more likely to become subsidy recipients.

Section 8 does offer some incentive to the individual household to find units renting for less than the FMR in the form of a "rent reduction credit" which is a fraction of the difference between the FMR and the actual rent. Over half the subsidized households are receiving this credit, which implies that over half of them are paying less than the FMR. Most of these households are being subsidized in place.

There are some administrative and technical problems with the program in its present form. The FMR and rent/income ratio limit, both features borrowed from the earlier housing programs, jointly act to limit the housing opportunities open to assisted families without facilitating program operation or reducing its cost. The maximum subsidy is the difference between the FMR and 25 percent of income. Households cannot live in a house or apartment renting for more than the FMR, even if they are willing to spend more than 25 percent of their own incomes to do so. Their options are limited, but the subsidy is not affected. Apparently, there have been a few instances in which the rent has been lowered to meet the FMR in order to qualify a unit for the program, but this slight downward pressure on rents is a small benefit and does not really change the amount of the subsidy but merely changes the specific housing unit on which the subsidy is paid.

The current system also gives rise to the possibility of kickbacks from tenant to landlord in cases where the tenant is willing to pay more than the allowed share of his or her income for the unit. The landlord can lower the contract rent to the FMR and can receive an additional payment from the tenant on the side. This is illegal, but it would be very hard to detect since it is mutually beneficial to the landlord and the tenant.

Program Costs. The costs are comparatively low, but have been rising. As of 1976 the monthly subsidy paid by the government was $103. (This is much less than would be paid under any recent new construction subsidy program, including Sections 235 and 236, which subsidized higher income groups.) The budget for fiscal 1981 projects a much higher monthly subsidy of $250. This figure is unadjusted for future inflation. Calculations of the Congressional Budget Office indicate that costs will range from about $250 to $330 per month, depending on the rate of inflation.[54] In constant dollars, new construction costs one-third to one-half more than existing housing, and the difference of course widens when nominal costs are compared. The 1980 federal budget promised that, in order to hold program

---

[54] Congressional Budget Office, *Long-Term Costs of Housing Programs,* pp. 21–25.

costs down, efforts would be made to encourage greater reliance on the existing stock of housing to aid the poor,[55] but the 1981 budget showed no appreciable change from earlier years.

Despite its relatively low cost the program is sometimes attacked as being too expensive. A report by the U.S. General Accounting Office calculated that Section 8 existing housing would cost more to subsidize than public housing over a twenty-to-forty-year period (the life of the subsidy on new units) because the mortgage rate on the new construction, which determines the subsidy, is fixed, while the rents on existing units can be expected to rise with inflation.[56] This conclusion holds only if inflation is not accurately forecast by mortgage lenders and bondholders, so that they accept interest rates which will give them a low or a negative real return on their money.

Part of the criticism of Section 8 existing housing arises from the strong preference of many housing specialists and program administrators for building new housing, both because it stimulates the housing industry and because it is regarded as "better" for the poor. The program is viewed somewhat unfavorably because it does not directly produce more housing, and there are efforts to modify it. Thus, the current administration has created a subcategory of the program known as "Section 8 moderate rehabilitation." Under this subcategory tenants will receive Section 8 subsidies after the housing has been upgraded to meet program standards. The program may well be used to finance the improvements directly: the 1980 budget states that "allowable rents under Section 8 may be adjusted to reflect reasonable costs attributable to moderate unit upgrading."[57] In Section 8 existing housing the subsidy does not depend on the extent of housing improvement or expenditure by the landlord. The 1981 budget authorizes monthly subsidies of $350, $100 more than for apartments in the existing program.

Evidence of the high cost of Section 8 existing units is given prominent attention in the housing trade press. One such story reported HUD calculations of costs for Section 8 and public housing in fiscal 1979, purporting to show that new public housing is less expensive than existing Section 8 housing in half the HUD area offices.[58] Later in the story the reporter noted that the public housing cost

---

[55] Office of Management and Budget, *U.S. 1980 Budget*, p. 261.

[56] U.S. General Accounting Office, *A Comparative Analysis of Subsidized Housing Costs*, staff paper, July 1976, chap. 4.

[57] Department of Housing and Urban Development, *1980 HUD Budget Summary*, p. H–3.

[58] "New Public Housing Takes Less Subsidy Than Sec. 8 Existing in 24 HUD Offices," *Housing Affairs Letter*, January 19, 1979, p. 3.

omitted operating subsidies, while the Section 8 calculations assumed that tenants contributed nothing toward the rent, implying that they have no income. Thus, the comparisons were biased, since a public housing tenant requiring no operating subsidy would have a relatively high income. The calculations also omitted tax benefits and other indirect subsidies, which are greater in public housing. The budgetary purpose of HUD cost calculations is to indicate the maximum subsidy that might be required, and operating subsidies for public housing are in a different budget category from debt service on new units.

Section 8 existing housing is not only less expensive than public housing—it appears to be more desirable. A 1976 HUD field survey found a number of local housing authorities that were concerned that public housing tenants would seek to take advantage of Section 8 subsidies to move to better privately owned housing, leaving the authorities with vacant units and difficulties in meeting debt service on their bonds.[59] So far, however, this fear has proved groundless, perhaps because there is so much excess demand for Section 8 subsidies that local authorities have been able to exclude public housing tenants.

Section 8 Loan Management and Property Disposition

Included under Section 8 existing housing, but quite different from it in spirit, purpose, and operation, is a program that provides subsidies to tenants in financially distressed housing projects insured by HUD under its earlier programs—primarily Sections 221 (d) (3) and 236. This is known as "Section 8 loan management and property disposition." It functions much like the subsidies for new housing in that the subsidy is tied to the unit, although it is based on the income of the occupant. When the occupant leaves, he or she loses the subsidy and must reapply for it. Not more than 40 percent of the apartments in a project can be subsidized by Section 8.

This program began in 1976 with 30,000 units; 80,000 more were subsidized in 1977. These represented more than 10 percent of all Section 221 and Section 236 units. The program added only 22,000 units in 1978, and is being phased out in fiscal year 1980. However, it does not include all of the financially distressed projects. A new

---

[59] Department of Housing and Urban Development, *Section 8: Existing Housing,* p. 41. A mathematical analysis of the likely extent of this phenomenon is provided in Michael P. Murray, "A Potential Hazard of Housing Allowances for Public Housing," *Journal of Urban Economics,* vol. 4 (April 1977), pp. 119–34.

"troubled projects program" was established in the 1979 budget, providing flexible subsidies, based on the income of tenants, to projects that are having trouble meeting debt service and operating expenses. In the first two years of operation, HUD proposes to assist between 4,300 and 6,300 projects; the total is uncertain because up to 2,000 projects will receive funding in both years. There are about 10,000 eligible projects; thus, perhaps half of all Section 221 and Section 236 apartments will receive subsidies as "troubled projects," in addition to the interest rate subsidies they are already receiving.

The Section 8 loan management program is thus basically a way of bailing out projects insured in the older programs to prevent default and foreclosure. The program is also being used to persuade private firms to buy HUD-owned projects that have already been foreclosed, by promising that some of the apartments will be subsidized and thus that the buyer will have a guaranteed rent. The program is essentially mislabeled. It is an additional subsidy to now defunct programs, not a means of helping low-income families live in decent privately owned housing without spending too much of their income on rent.

5

Potential Alternatives

Two alternative program approaches that have attracted serious attention in recent years are discussed in this chapter. While neither approach is currently under active consideration, one or both may attract renewed attention in the future if any of the more serious potential problems of the present programs materialize.

Housing Allowances

At the time that Section 8 was enacted it appeared to be a possible precursor of a system of housing allowances which would be closer to an unrestricted cash transfer. As in Section 8, payments would be made to individuals and families, earmarked for their housing expenses, but fewer restrictions would be placed on the uses of the funds, and landlords would not participate directly in the program at all.

Background. Housing allowances have been considered and discussed in virtually every major debate on housing policy since the Housing Act of 1937 established public housing.[1] Generally, allowances were rejected on the grounds of administrative complexity and budget outlay, and because of more substantive criticisms to the effect that recipients would be degraded by receiving assistance in such a form and that the program would not add to the supply of housing but would merely drive up rents, leaving the poor no better off.

The first significant policy shifts came in 1965, when rent supplements and Section 23 were enacted over the traditional objections. Shortly thereafter, the President's Committee on Urban Housing (the Kaiser Committee) recommended that an experiment be undertaken

---

[1] U.S. Department of Housing and Urban Development, Office of Policy Development and Research, *Housing Allowances: The 1976 Report to Congress*, 1976, appendix I.

to test the effects of allowances. Legislative authority for the experiment was provided in 1970. In the interim, model cities programs in Kansas City, Missouri, and Wilmington, Delaware, had begun demonstrations on their own initiative. By 1973 the Experimental Housing Allowance Program (EHAP) was getting under way after a two-year development process: as yet there were no research results that could be used in policy formulation. The National Housing Policy Review recommended against such a program until more information was available. In his message to Congress, President Nixon termed housing allowances "the most promising way to achieve decent housing for all of our families at an acceptable cost,"[2] and indicated that he expected to make a final decision late in 1974 or early in 1975 on whether to recommend a housing allowance program. A report on the experiments, with policy recommendations, was prepared by HUD in 1974, but the experiments were still continuing at that time— indeed, the largest components of EHAP were still getting under way—and President Ford did not present a new proposal to Congress.

Experimental Housing Allowance Program. EHAP, the largest social experiment yet undertaken by the federal government, is scheduled to continue over a period of ten years and to include over 20,000 households at twelve different locations around the country. It consists of three separate but interrelated components: (1) the Demand Experiment, which studies the effects of different assistance formulas on the housing decisions of recipients; (2) the Supply Experiment, which offers assistance to every eligible family in an SMSA and investigates the impact on the recipients and on the housing market as a whole; and (3) the Administrative Agency Experiment (AAE), which compares the costs and problems of using various administrative mechanisms for a program on the local level.

The Supply Experiment is by far the largest. It comprises some 6,800 households in Green Bay, Wisconsin, and 10,000 in South Bend, Indiana, that are offered subsidies over a five-year experimental period (assuming continued eligibility) and for five years beyond that period, in an effort to induce them to treat the funds as permanent rather than transitory income. Both homeowners and renters are aided. In contrast, the Demand Experiment comprises about 1,200 renters apiece in Pittsburgh, Pennsylvania, and Phoenix, Arizona, who are subsidized for three years with some subsequent assistance; and the Administrative Agency Experiment provides support to be-

---

[2] Message of President Nixon to Congress, September 19, 1973, p. 9.

tween 400 and 900 renters, at each of eight locations, for two years. At present only the two Supply Experiments (which were begun in 1974) are continuing to operate; the other two experiments were completed during 1976 and early 1977.

Three of the research subjects studied in EHAP are particularly important in the context of housing policy: (1) the effect of the program on the housing market, particularly the changes in the quality of housing occupied by the recipients and the price they pay for it; (2) the extent to which the recipients use their payments to improve their housing rather than to increase their expenditures on other goods and services; and (3) the locational effects, especially the changes in racial segregation and neighborhood stability.

The Supply Experiment was designed to focus on the first subject.[3] After the first three years of the experiment in Green Bay and the first two in South Bend, the analysts evaluating the results concluded: "The evidence to date indicates that the attempts of program participants to secure acceptable housing have had virtually no effect on rents or home prices in either site, but have resulted in a modest improvement in the quality of existing housing."[4] There is little evidence of rent increases for assisted households, for other low-income households, or in the housing market generally. Green Bay, a rapidly growing area, has been a chronically tight housing market with a persistently low vacancy rate. In the first three years of the experiment rents rose by less than 5 percent annually. In South Bend, where vacancy rates are higher and there is little growth, rents increased by about 3 percent per year during the first eighteen months. These market-wide increases are remarkably small. The experiment provided subsidy to low-income households whose housing was of standard quality; subsidized renters in both areas reported still lower rates of rent increase, indicating that landlords did not take advantage of the subsidies.

The Supply Experiment staff evaluates the dwelling of each household when it enrolls in the experiment to determine whether the unit meets the quality standards established for assistance. These standards are based on model housing codes devised by professionals in public health. About half the eligible households (51 percent in Green Bay and 45 percent in South Bend) lived in acceptable housing. In both areas, slightly more than two-thirds of those living in unac-

---

[3] Unless other sources are indicated, information on the housing allowance experiments is taken from RAND Corporation, *Fourth Annual Report of the Housing Assistance Supply Experiment* (Santa Monica, Calif.: RAND Corporation, 1978).
[4] Ibid., pp. xv–xvi.

ceptable housing upgraded their housing to meet the standards. Another 10 percent moved and the remainder dropped out of the program.

The expenditures required to bring the units up to standard were remarkably small: the median was about $10 per unit in each city, with 75 percent spending less than $25 in Green Bay and less than $30 in South Bend. These figures, however, probably understate the actual level of outlays, because they are either reported by the tenant or estimated by the interviewer; in the former case, at least, they are likely to be underestimates of the landlord's expenditures. Another consideration is that repairs were generally performed by the landlord, the tenant, the homeowner, or their friends. Half the renters and two-thirds of the homeowners did the work themselves in Green Bay. The figures were somewhat smaller in South Bend, in part, at least, because those assisted were more frequently elderly single persons or households headed by women. The dollar outlay figures, then, significantly understate the market value of the improvement since they do not include the value of the labor provided. These qualifications should not be overemphasized, however. The most common repairs were small ones, such as repairing windows or doors and installing handrails on stairways; the market value of such repairs cannot be very high. Both the outlays and the nature of the repairs indicate that the low-income housing was adequate, or nearly so.

Housing is reevaluated a year after it has initially been improved. At this point in the Supply Experiment, about 20 percent of the units in Green Bay and 40 percent in South Bend had deteriorated to the point of being substandard. Most of these—perhaps 90 percent—were repaired to meet the standards of the experiment and to permit continued occupancy by the recipients. The outlays apparently were about the same as the amounts required to upgrade the dwellings that had failed initially to qualify.[5] In addition, during the year about 42 percent of renters and 72 percent of owners made voluntary repairs. These voluntary repairs typically involved major structural work or substantial repairs to the basic utility systems and were therefore more expensive than the repairs originally made to meet the program standards; the median outlay was $65 for renters and $210 for owners in Green Bay, and $75 and $250 in South Bend. Professional contractors were employed on about one-quarter of these repair jobs (half for South Bend owners). The expenditures were much

---

[5] The data do not separate the outlays for these two purposes, but information on the distribution of outlays indicates that it is very unlikely that they differed substantially, or that outlays for reevaluated units were very large.

greater for recipient homeowners than for homeowners with similar incomes who were not participating in the experiment.

From these results it appears that the subsidies are sufficient to encourage the recipients to improve their housing to the relatively minor extent required in most cases, and to maintain it in satisfactory condition.

Both the Demand and the Supply Experiments provide evidence of the extent to which families increase their expenditure for housing in relation to that for other goods. Generally, expenditure increases for housing are small, except in the case of those households that are required or that choose to move as a result of the assistance.

As has been mentioned, renters remaining in the same units reported insignificant rent increases in Green Bay and South Bend. These renters chose to spend virtually all of their allowance payment on other goods. One reason for this behavior is undoubtedly that 90 percent had been spending more than one-quarter of their income for rent. With the help of subsidy they were able to cut their rent burdens substantially, so that about 65 percent had rent/income ratios above 0.25. If a high rent burden is regarded as a form of housing inadequacy, as some housing analysts have recently claimed,[6] then a quarter of the renters in the experiment remedied the deficiency. Among owners the improvement was more dramatic: the percentage with a housing expense/income ratio above 0.25 fell from three-quarters to one-quarter of the participants.

Not all households chose to reduce their housing expense burden. Some 700 households in Green Bay and 300 in South Bend moved *after* their residences were judged acceptable by program standards, which suggests that they chose to improve their housing significantly with their increased financial resources. These households comprise about 10 percent of actively participating households in Green Bay and 3 percent in South Bend. Renters in this group reported average increases of 23 percent and 32 percent, respectively. Increases of nearly 50 percent were reported by those renters in both areas who moved when their initial residences failed to meet the quality standards.

These results appear to indicate that most households do not choose to increase their housing expenditures significantly unless they are required to do so to qualify for the subsidy. It should be noted, however, that the results cover a relatively short period of time. Economists who have analyzed housing market behavior over

---

[6] David Birch et al., *America's Housing Needs: 1970 to 1980* (Cambridge, Mass.: Joint Center for Urban Studies, 1973), p. 213.

the past two decades have found that many, if not most, households generally do not move immediately or otherwise adjust their housing quality and expenditures to an increase in their income. It is possible that both mobility and housing expenditures will increase to a greater extent as the experiment continues.

The subsidy cost of a full-scale housing allowance program has been estimated at about $90 per household per month on the basis of the experiences in Green Bay and South Bend. This is about 10 percent less than the costs of the Section 8 existing program. At the same time, the difference should not be given undue attention: it may not be possible to generalize from the experience of these two smaller midwestern metropolitan areas to large areas in other parts of the country, or to small towns and rural areas. It seems clear, however, that the costs of subsidizing the poor to live in existing housing, by either means, will be much lower than the costs of building new housing for them.

Effect on Neighborhoods. One of the major political concerns over housing allowances has been their effect on racial integration and neighborhood stability. To date, evidence from the two supply sites suggests little effect on residential patterns by race. In South Bend nearly all of the black participants and half of the whites originally lived in the central part of the city. There was no net racial change in this area among participants; larger families of both races tended to move out and to be replaced by young single persons or childless couples. Within the area the research staff noted some dispersion of blacks and movement of whites from predominantly black census tracts. The analysts concluded that "the program may have speeded the normal process of black dispersion, but not dramatically. White flight may have been facilitated, but not very much."[7]

In the AAE sites there is some tendency for black households to move to areas with greater integration: the incidence of blacks in the census tracts containing their new residences was 40 percent compared with 56 percent in the initial tracts.[8] In addition, the socioeconomic status of residents in the new tracts was typically higher; however, over one-quarter of the black movers went to tracts with lower status.

Among Spanish-Americans in the AAE sites, half moved; the

---

[7] RAND, *Fourth Annual Report*, p. 133.
[8] Abt Associates, *Third Annual Report, Administrative Agency Evaluation* (Cambridge, Mass.: Abt Associates, 1976), pp. 59–62.

incidence of Hispanics by tract was not identified, but the socioeconomic status and the percentage of minority residents were virtually unchanged.

Attitudes toward Program Results. The experimental findings to date indicate that housing allowances generate relatively little improvement in housing unless standards are adopted that require upgrading for receipt of the subsidy. Builders and housing advocates have therefore generally been antipathetic toward the concept of a housing allowance, and it has become less popular as a policy option in recent years. In Senate hearings during the fall of 1978 the HUD officials responsible for managing the experiment argued that it had shown that housing allowances would not "work," because little housing would be built or substantially rehabilitated and low-income families would not improve their housing conditions. The benefits accruing to low-income families from a lower rent burden and a higher standard of living generally were minimized.[9] Such an argument must be based on the premise that the poor should not be allowed to choose how they wish to spend their money, an assumption that is repugnant in a democratic society; or it must be based on the argument that housing produces positive externalities, which are not accurately valued in the market. So far, as noted in chapter 1, there is little evidence that such externalities exist or have any importance.

The housing allowance program is also criticized because it has not increased the extent of racial integration. This represents a remarkable reversal of attitude: originally the program was attacked because it *would* increase integration.

HUD's attitude toward its own experiment may result in part from the 1977 proposal by the U.S. Department of Health, Education, and Welfare (HEW) to fold the housing subsidy programs into general welfare reform. The current housing allowance experiments are operating in many respects as unrestricted income transfers, and it is difficult to argue in favor of allowances and against unrestricted transfers at the same time. The HEW proposal would have reduced drastically both HUD's budget and its justification. Before this interagency dispute, HUD Secretary Patricia Roberts Harris had spoken favorably about housing allowances at her Senate confirmation hearing.[10]

---

[9] Spencer Rich, "No-Strings Housing Subsidy Is Faulted," *Washington Post*, November 17, 1978, p. A9.
[10] U.S. Congress, Senate, Committee on Banking, Housing, and Urban Affairs, *Nomination Hearings*, 95th Cong., 1st sess., January 20, 1977, p. 26.

Housing Block Grants

Another option considered as a replacement for the suspended subsidy programs during the 1973 moratorium was a housing block grant similar to the Community Development Block Grant (CDBG) then in the process of being enacted. The Domestic Council recommended such a program to President Nixon. Simultaneously, Congressmen William A. Barrett (D-Pa.) and Thomas L. Ashley (D-Ohio) introduced a bill to replace public housing, Section 235 and Section 236, with block grants. Funds were to be distributed to localities on the basis of population, housing overcrowding, and poverty (the last being given double weight); the localities could spend the money in any of a wide variety of ways, including for activities not covered in the three programs being supplanted. Senator John Sparkman (D-Ala.) introduced similar but less sweeping legislation. Congressman Barrett and Senator Sparkman were the chairmen of the congressional housing subcommittees, and Congressman Ashley was a recognized authority on housing; the concept had strong support. Interest in block grants waned, however, after President Nixon proposed the expanded Section 23 leased public housing program (enacted as Section 8) and indicated his support for housing allowances.

By 1976 the Ford administration's experience with Section 8, particularly with congressional restrictions on the allocation of new and existing units to individual localities, generated renewed interest in block grants. A modified block grant was proposed in President Ford's last budget, but it was not favored by the incoming Carter administration and was dropped in President Carter's budget revisions. Thus, somewhat ironically, the two parties had switched positions in the space of about four years.

The Ford block grant proposal was narrower than the earlier versions had been, at least initially.[11] It comprised only the Section 8 program and allocated the dollar amount of budget authority for Section 8 to individual localities, leaving them the choice of how to split the money among new, rehabilitated, and existing housing. The current Section 8 allocation system is rather similar. Localities indicate their preferences for the three types of housing in the Housing Assistance Plans (HAPs), and HUD is required by congressional mandate to allocate Section 8 units in accordance with the HAPs, so that in both instances the choice of mix would be left to the locality.

However, the block grant changed the incentives confronting the

---

[11] U.S. Department of Housing and Urban Development, *Summary of the HUD Budget, Fiscal Year 1978*, 1977, p. H–2.

90

locality. Under Section 8 the trade-off between new and existing units is essentially one-for-one; the overall number of assisted units is based on the HAP and a locality can vary the mix within the overall level. In contrast, under the block grant proposal the dollar volume of budget authority was fixed and differing subsidy amounts were available for the different types of units. Since existing housing would require about half as much budget authority per unit, the locality could now get two more existing units for every new unit forgone. The higher "price" of subsidized new housing could have been expected to result in an increased reliance on existing units to house the poor.

The block grant would also have modified the administration of Section 8 significantly. The congressional requirement that Section 8 assistance be provided in accordance with the HAPs gave the locality the authority to choose the form of assistance but left HUD with the responsibility of producing the housing. The block grant would have given both the authority and the responsibility to the locality.

The proposed Section 8 block grant was viewed by the administration as a first step toward a broader housing block grant similar to the Barrett-Ashley proposal. After a three-year trial period the administration proposed permitting localities to design their own forms of housing assistance to meet local market situations; it was hoped that the block grant would, in this way, foster innovative local program ideas. Thus, if implemented, the grant would eventually probably overlap with Community Development Block Grants, which are being used for a variety of housing subsidies, including several that resemble the options included in the Barrett-Ashley proposal. There would be differences in coverage: CDBG funds are commonly used in specific neighborhoods and may assist middle-income families and even middle-income neighborhoods, while the housing block grants would be limited to families with lower incomes (80 percent of the locality's median income in the Barrett-Ashley bill).

6

Homeownership: A Fading Dream?

The rising prices of homes, particularly of new homes, have attracted national attention in recent years, to the point of being the subject of a *Time* magazine cover story.[1] The basic price figures are frightening: the typical new home in 1979 cost more than 2½ times the typical 1970 new home—$62,900 versus $23,400. Resale prices of existing homes rose a little less sharply, but still more than doubled, to $55,700 from $23,000. These increases have evoked fears that many, if not most, potential home buyers are being priced out of the market, or soon will be. A 1977 study of housing received major news media coverage when it extrapolated the preceding five years' new home price increase over the next five years, showing that the 1981 median price would be $78,000 if the past trend were to continue.[2]

The concern over costs has become the current central focus of the long-standing federal policies of encouraging homeownership and home building. This concern has generated legislative proposals and recommendations from industry groups and housing analysts to bring homeownership within the reach of the middle-income and young families believed to be most severely affected by the price increases. In addition, policy analyses of other urban issues increasingly begin with the assumption that fewer families can afford to buy a house, and go on from there to develop recommendations.[3]

But at the same time that prices have been rising, sales have been rising as well, and at almost the same rate. The 1979 sales volumes

---

[1] "Housing: It's Outasight," *Time*, vol. 110 (September 12, 1977), pp. 50–54.
[2] Bernard J. Frieden and Arthur P. Solomon, *The Nation's Housing: 1975–1985* (Cambridge, Mass.: Joint Center for Urban Studies, 1977), p. 116.
[3] For example, see Stephen R. Seidel, *Housing Costs and Government Regulations: Confronting the Regulatory Maze* (New Brunswick, N.J.: Rutgers University, Center for Urban Policy Research, 1978), especially chap. 2.

for both new and existing homes were about double the 1970 rates. Some 712,000 new homes and 3.75 million existing homes were sold, in comparison with 418,000 and 1.6 million, respectively, nine years earlier.

The existing home sales volume was less than 1 percent below the record of 3.9 million established in 1978, while new home sales were about 100,000 units, or 13 percent, below the 1977 peak; the 712,000 total was the fourth highest year on record. During the 1970s the proportion of homeowners in the population rose steadily, from 63 to 65 percent—which is double the rate of increase for the 1960s.

The combination of rising prices and record sales has been remarked by several analysts. A frequent explanation is that demographic changes have created the sales activity. The children of the postwar baby boom are now in the prime home-buying age brackets of the late twenties and early thirties, and there are so many of them that records are being set in spite of price increases. In this view the sales volume is a transitory phenomenon and is misleading, since many young families, in particular, are thought to be priced out of the housing market. Rising prices are believed to be a major new problem, even though many people are buying homes.[4]

This explanation overlooks the historical patterns in both housing policy and housing markets. It is also inconsistent with the available data on the actual behavior of home buyers in recent years. The "major new problem" of rapidly rising prices driving many families out of the housing market is in fact neither new nor a major problem. Similar concerns have been voiced continually over several decades. To the extent that homes are becoming less affordable, the problem is generated primarily by rising mortgage interest rates, not rising prices, and both are basically manifestations of the general inflation in the American economy during the past decade or more.

Other expenses of operating a home, notably the costs of fuel and utilities, have also been increasing, but none of these factors has been serious enough to limit significantly the ability of American families to buy homes. Most already own a home and are able to buy a better one with the increased value of their current residence. Homeownership has been the best hedge against inflation readily available in recent years, and even young families without the capital gains from a previous home have been buying more frequently than their predecessors did, in an attempt to protect themselves against inflation. These young families, however, are not putting unusual financial pressure on themselves to do so.

---

[4] Frieden and Solomon, *Nation's Housing*, pp. 112–13.

Policy proposals intended to deal with the problem of housing prices frequently fail to focus on its source and usually underestimate the extent of ownership and the current rate of home purchase. Thus, these proposals are likely to be ineffective or expensive, or both. However, some things can be done, and are being done, to ameliorate the special problems created for home buyers by inflation.

The discussion in this chapter refers primarily to the market for new homes, although the argument is applicable in large part also to resales of existing homes. More data are available on new homes and many suggested policies for bringing down the cost of housing are restricted to new homes.

Housing Costs in Historical Perspective

Public concern over high prices dates back at least to the Great Depression, at which time the earliest steps were taken toward developing a federal policy to encourage homeownership. In the hearings preceding the enactment of the National Housing Act of 1937 many witnesses cited the high cost of new housing as justification for the public housing program. In the words of Catherine Bauer, widely recognized as one of the leading housing analysts in the country:

> The major part of the housing problem is a simple economic fact: Ordinary private enterprise is totally unable to provide adequate new housing at a rental or sale price which families in the middle and lower income groups can pay. This situation is apparently permanent in our economy.[5]

Because of the cost problem, Bauer and other witnesses rejected the notion of rent subsidies, which was then espoused by the U.S. Chamber of Commerce.

Throughout the depression and through World War II the same situation was frequently perceived. The Temporary National Economic Committee concluded in 1938 that very few families could afford the kind of homes then being built. More than 80 percent of these homes were selling for $4,000 or more, while only 24 percent of families had the $2,000 income thought necessary for such a house.[6] At the end of the war the Senate Special Committee on Postwar Economic Policy and Planning again reviewed the housing situation

---

[5] Testimony of Catherine Bauer, in U.S. Congress, Senate, Committee on Education and Labor, *Hearings on S. 2392,* 74th Cong., 1st sess., June 1935, p. 86.

[6] U.S. Temporary National Economic Committee, *Toward More Housing,* Monograph No. 8, U.S. Congress, Senate, 76th Cong., 2nd sess., 1940, pp. 24–25.

and called for "a better balance between housing cost and family income."[7]

Statements of concern continued to be heard after the war, but with a new twist: housing prices were not only high but were rising rapidly, and therefore it was becoming harder for families to buy new homes than it used to be. The congressional Joint Committee on Housing, conducting hearings around the nation in 1947 and 1948, heard complaints such as that of a United Automobile Workers official in St. Louis:

> Before the end of 1946, the building industry was again starting to price itself out of the market. During the months of 1947 it has done a good job of completing the process—with building costs at a record high—with virtually no homes even being planned for those of average income, to say nothing of those in the lower income brackets. . . . 1946 was a good construction year. More new building units were started in 1946 than in any other previous year. At the start of 1947, it was hoped that construction activity would exceed even that of 1946. However, for the first four months of 1947, as we can see by reports, fewer new dwelling units were started than in the same months of 1946. . . . The reason for the decline, according to the Federal Reserve Board in its June bulletin, is that the rise in prices was greater, and resistance to them stiffer, than had been estimated. . . . As the Board points out, prices of housing and real estate are too high to support the present boom market. . . . The average house on the market today sells for far more than these families can afford to pay.[8]

Academic analysts saw the same problem. "The spread between what housing costs and what American families can pay for it has increased since the war," Edward Weinfeld wrote in 1949. "Not only are the lowest reaches of the income level outside the market for housing today, but the great middle segment also is experiencing great difficulty in finding housing at prices it can pay," Weinfeld continued. "Indeed, nearly 70 percent of American families have incomes below $4,000 a year, the amount needed to buy the cheapest of the housing commonly being produced today."[9]

---

[7] U.S. Congress, Senate, Special Committee on Postwar Economic Policy and Planning, Subcommittee on Housing and Urban Development, *Report: Postwar Housing*, 79th Cong., 1st sess., August 1945.
[8] Testimony of Luther Slinkard, in U.S. Congress, Joint Committee on Housing, *Study and Investigation of Housing*, 80th Cong., 1st sess., July 1947, part 1, pp. 708–9.
[9] Edward Weinfeld, "Can America Be Adequately Housed?" *American Journal of Economics and Sociology*, vol. 49 (October 1949), pp. 83–84.

Some 15 years later, Bernard J. Frieden saw the same problem:

> The cost of new housing today prices most American families
> out of the market. By the end of 1965, the median sales price
> of new single-family houses had risen to $20,000. Sixty-five
> percent of all new homes sold for $17,500 or more, and only
> 9 percent for under $12,500. Ownership of new homes is
> effectively limited to the top quarter of American families,
> who earn $8,000 a year or more.[10]

But from the perspective of a decade later, the situation in the mid-
1960s did not appear to be as bad. Writing in 1977, Frieden and
coauthor Arthur Solomon concluded that:

> Although new homes were too expensive even then [from
> mid-1965 to mid-1966] for the very poor, families earning
> well below the median income were still represented. . . .
> Ten years later, from mid-1975 to mid-1976, home building
> was no longer primarily for the massive middle-income mar-
> ket. . . . Now the top fourth, earning $20,000 and more,
> dominated the market.[11]

If these analysts are right, it has become increasingly more difficult
to afford a new home since at least the war, and perhaps since the
depression, which must be a unique situation among consumer
goods. Moreover, production and homeownership have been going
up as affordability has been going down: more houses were built in
each year since the war than in any year on record before 1946, and
the proportion of homeowners in the population has similarly been
higher in every postwar year for which we have data than in any
prewar year. Ownership has been increasing steadily since 1950.

The Effect of Inflation on Housing

The key to this paradox of declining affordability juxtaposed with
increasing production and homeownership is the rate of inflation.
The latter half of the 1970s has seen the most rapid rate of price
increase in our peacetime history, but both the mid-1960s and late
1940s were periods of unusually rapid inflation by the standards and
experience of the times. The rate of increase of the Consumer Price
Index was about 8 percent in the immediate postwar period, in com-

---

[10] Bernard J. Frieden, "Housing and National Urban Goals: Old Policies and New
Realities," in James Q. Wilson, ed., *The Metropolitan Enigma* (Cambridge, Mass.: Har-
vard University Press, 1968), pp. 187–88. The papers in this volume were originally
written for a lecture series in 1966.
[11] Frieden and Solomon, *Nation's Housing*, pp. 106–7.

parison with 2 to 3 percent during the war. In the mid-1960s, it increased abruptly from 1.5 to 3 percent; in the mid-1970s, from 5 to 10 percent.

Inflation has several important effects on the housing market, some of which reduce the ability of American families to buy new homes, while others increase it. Moreover, the various effects interact with each other in complicated ways. It is worthwhile to disentangle them.

The most obvious effect is that inflation drives up the prices of new homes. This is the main reason for public concern. From 1967 to 1977, the typical new home sold increased in price by 115 percent.[12] This is an annual increase of 8 percent, compounded.

Such an increase is large enough for concern, but it is not unique to housing, unfortunately. Other commodities and services, such as fuels and utilities, showed similar increases. However, inflation has another deleterious effect which is especially important to home buyers: it drives up interest rates, including the mortgage rate, as lenders seek to protect the value of the dollars they will receive in future repayment of loans made today.

The rise in interest rates compounds the problem of buying a home. In 1967, when the typical new home cost $22,700, the mortgage interest rate was about 6 percent, and inflation was about 3 percent. The monthly mortgage payment for a typical buyer was $110, after a 25 percent down payment. In 1977, the typical home cost $48,800, the interest rate had risen to 9 percent, and inflation was about 6 percent. With the same down payment, the monthly mortgage payment would have been about $307, an increase of 182 percent from a decade earlier. Three-quarters of the increase occurred because of the increase in home prices, the remaining quarter because of the interest rate rise. Even though the interest rate increase is quantitatively less important than the price rise, it is the more significant determinant of affordability and housing market behavior. Its importance was exemplified in late 1979 and early 1980, a period in which new home prices stabilized and actually declined slightly, but interest rates continued to rise sharply. Sales volume responded to interest rates rather than prices and fell markedly. This behavior conformed to the general historical pattern: sales and prices both tend to decline when mortgage rates rise.

With cost increases of this order of magnitude, it may be hard

---

[12] The comparisons in this subsection conclude with the year 1978 because all of the data required for 1979 is not available at this writing. It seems clear, however, that the trends reported in the text have not changed.

to see how very many people can afford to buy a house. However, inflation has offsetting effects. The income of the typical family, for example, rose by 102 percent in the 1967–1977 decade, or 7.25 percent annually, compounded. The rates of increase have been about the same for both before- and after-tax income.

This is almost, though not quite, as rapid a rate of growth as that of new home prices, but it has attracted much less attention among housing analysts. One reason for the greater attention given to house prices is the sequence in which data become available. Each year, prices and incomes have increased in roughly the same proportion. But the price increases are reported each month, with about a month's lag; the income data are reported only once a year, at least nine months after the end of the year. We already know that the median new home price in 1979 was $62,900, a record high; we do not, at this writing, know what the median income was. The latest income data, which became available in November 1979, are for 1978. There are thus no detailed income data for comparison to prices, and there will not be until late 1980, when new home prices will again be higher.[13] In a period of stable prices, the lag is not especially important; in a period of inflation, it can contribute to a misleading impression of what is happening in the housing market.

Inflation has one other important effect: it drives up the prices of existing homes, as well as new ones. The typical existing home in 1977 sold for $42,900, up 121 percent from $19,400 in 1967. This increase in existing home prices is important to an understanding of the ability of American families to upgrade their housing and buy new homes. The increase is bad for those families who rent and want to buy; it indicates that any house, new or existing, has probably more than doubled in price, and is now more expensive, relative to their income. But it is good for those families who already own a home, when they want to buy another one, and these families are the majority of the population. Over 60 percent of American households have owned their own homes during the 1960s and 1970s and the proportion has been steadily rising. Current homeowners form a substantial part of the market for new homes (or existing homes, for that matter). When seeking to buy another home, the current owner faces the same inflation-induced price and interest rate in-

---

[13] Some income data, such as per capita income and disposable income, are available monthly on a timely basis. These figures, however, do not include any measures of the distribution of income and do not refer to families or households. Housing analysts have usually been interested in distributional measures, so that they can calculate the percentage of families that can hypothetically afford to buy the median-priced new home or some other specified type of housing.

creases as the renter, but the homeowner has the advantage that his or her current home has increased in value, again as a result of inflation. The homeowner has thus hedged against inflation in the housing market. Indeed, the homeowner has more than hedged, since the entire increase in the value of the home accrues to him or her as equity: for most homeowners, the mortgage balance and interest rate are unchanged by inflation.

The effect of inflation on the homeowner may be illustrated by the following analysis of the typical 1968 new home buyer's position in the 1978 market. After putting 25 percent down on a $25,000 home, the typical buyer had an $18,750 mortgage for twenty-five years. Including taxes, utilities, and other operating costs, the buyer would have spent about $2,475 per year on housing. According to the rule of thumb that housing expenses should not exceed 25 percent of income, the buyer would have needed to earn about $9,900 yearly. By 1978, if we assume, conservatively, that the value of the home has risen by 120 percent, the buyer's equity would have increased more than six times.[14] The buyer would have paid off $3,900 on the mortgage (about 21 percent) and would have an equity of over $40,000 in his or her $55,000 home. This becomes a down payment on a new home. On the additional conservative assumption that the 1968 buyer remains in the same position in the income distribution over the ten-year period, his or her 1978 income would be about $21,000, which would permit a monthly housing expense of about $440 under the 25 percent rule of thumb. For that outlay the buyer can meet the mortgage payment and operating costs on a $64,000 house. The value of the new home is much higher in relation to the buyer's income than the old one was when he or she bought it, but the buyer can afford the new one because the mortgage principal is only about $24,000.

This new home would be in the upper half of the price distribution in 1978; thus, the home buyer would have bettered himself or herself, relatively speaking. What is more pertinent from the buyer's standpoint is that the new home would be substantially larger and better than the old one. The typical 1978 new home in the $60,000

---

[14] There is no price index for existing homes, so that any adjustment in value for inflation must be somewhat arbitrary. The longest series on existing home prices is compiled by the National Association of Realtors; it shows a 142 percent rise from 1968 to 1978. This series, like the Census Bureau's median new home price, is not adjusted for changes in size or amenities of homes sold. The Census Bureau's new home price index increased by 127 percent, from 1968 to 1978; this may be the best available approximation for the price inflation that has occurred in 1968 homes. The assumption used in the text is more conservative than either series mentioned here.

to $70,000 price range had over 1,800 square feet of floor space, some 200 more square feet than the typical 1968 home; it also had a larger garage, central air conditioning, and other amenities.

This is only one example, but it is typical of the calculations for other years. When the equity in the current home is taken into account, it appears that the typical homeowner is better off now than in past years, if he or she wishes to buy a new home.[15]

Underlying these calculations is a recognition that a home is both an item of consumption and an investment, and that the decision to buy a home is a decision to invest as well as consume. In recent years, housing analysts have increasingly recognized the investment aspect of homeownership and have attempted to measure the rate of return to the homeowner, viewed as an investor. Precise calculation of the return is complicated, since the expenditure must be compared with the rent that would be paid if the owner were a tenant in his or her own home, and this information must usually be inferred or estimated. But despite the difficulties, some empirical studies have been undertaken.

Their general conclusion can be stated simply: homeownership has proved to be a good investment, one of the very few that has produced a rate of return that keeps pace with inflation. For example, Hendershott and Hu calculate that owner-occupants have earned on average about 9 percent more annually than investors in financial assets over the period 1964–1978. Returns were higher than average after 1973, but were above those for other assets throughout the period.[16] Another study by the investment research department of Goldman, Sachs & Co. concludes that homeowners received a current yield of 8 percent on their homes in 1977 (ignoring anticipated future rent increases). This had been the lowest yield in the past twenty years. In addition, actual rents increased about 6 percent in 1977; if future increases were expected at the same rate, the anticipated rate of return would be about 14 percent. This is somewhat lower than anticipated returns over the last decade but is above those of earlier years. The calculations were based on estimates of the rental value of the home, operating costs, and marginal income tax rates for the typical home buyer, with the rent estimate having the most significant

[15] John C. Weicher, "New Home Affordability, Equity, and Housing Market Behavior," *AREUEA Journal*, vol. 6 (Winter 1978), pp. 395–416.
[16] Patric H. Hendershott and Sheng Cheng Hu, "Inflation and Extraordinary Returns on Owner-Occupied Housing: Some Implications for Economic Stability and Efficiency," paper presented at the Conference on Housing Prices and Inflation, Washington, D.C., April 3, 1980.

effect on the rate of return. The analysts concluded that new homes were not overpriced when viewed as investments by their buyers.[17]

This rate of return is increased by the interaction between inflation and the tax treatment of homeownership. Mortgage interest payments are deductible from personal income for tax purposes. Thus, if the mortgage rate is 9.5 percent, for example, as in 1978, then the after-tax rate of return is only about 6.5 percent for a family in the 32 percent tax bracket (income of about $30,000). With an inflation rate of about 7.6 percent, the real rate of interest, after taxes, is negative. In 1967, with a 6 percent interest rate and 3 percent inflation, a family in the same bracket would be paying about 1 percent in real terms (just over 4 percent nominally after taxes, less 3 percent inflation).

The tax treatment of homeownership in an inflationary period is especially favorable when compared with other investments. Feldstein and Summers have analyzed the impact of inflation on the tax paid by corporate capital and have found that the effective tax rate has risen by about half above the rate that would be paid in a noninflationary environment because of the tax rules on depreciation and inventory accounting procedures. These rules do not apply to residential real estate. Thus, investors are encouraged to put their money in real estate, particularly including their own home, rather than in manufacturing and other nonfinancial corporations.[18]

Changes in New Home Quality

The housing price figures cited in the preceding section are not adjusted to reflect changes in the quality of the typical new house over time. Instead, they are the median prices for the homes actually sold. Typically, each year new homes are slightly larger and have more amenities than the year before. During the period from 1963 to 1979, prices of new homes increased significantly more rapidly than did the cost of building the same houses. The average price increased by 262 percent, or 8.4 percent per year, in comparison with 214 percent, or 7.4 percent per year, from the Census Bureau's *Price Index of New One-Family Homes Sold*. This is the broadest home price index available in terms of market coverage and number of characteristics held con-

---

[17] Gary M. Wenglowski and Richard B. Worley, "Are Single-Family Homes Overpriced?" New York: Goldman, Sachs & Co., n.d.

[18] Martin Feldstein and Lawrence Summers, "Inflation and the Taxation of Capital Income in the Corporate Sector," Working Paper No. 312 (Cambridge, Mass.: National Bureau of Economic Research, January 1979).

stant.[19] The median sales price figures generally attract more attention from the press and housing policy makers, but they overstate the change in the cost of purchasing any particular house and mask the gradual but steady improvement that has occurred in housing quality. Since 1963, new home quality has improved by about 1.35 percent per year, on average. The rate of improvement seems to be stable; during the latest five years, it averaged about 1.65 percent, only slightly below the longer-term trend.

The improvement in housing quality may appear slight in comparison with the price increases. The latter, however, are primarily the result of the general inflation throughout the economy, rather than of any special cost problems in housing. Nearly 70 percent of the price increase for the typical new home during the 1968–1978 decade is accounted for by the overall rate of inflation, as measured by the Consumer Price Index. Of the remainder, about 20 percent consists of a rise in the price of homes relative to all other goods and services, and 10 percent represents quality improvement. Undoubtedly, it would be preferable if improvements in quality were greater and price increases smaller, but the rate of improvement is roughly consistent with the rate of increase in real income over the period.

Subsidized Production and Market Perceptions

Generally through this analysis of housing affordability we have used 1968 as the base year. Most recent discussions have used 1970. The latter is an obvious benchmark for trends in housing as in other aspects of life, since it was the beginning of a decade, but comparisons based on it give a misleading picture of recent trends, because it was also the first year of substantial new home production under the Section 235 and Section 502 subsidy programs. Under Section 235, as described in chapter 4, low-income families received subsidies to enable them to buy either new or existing homes. The program was enacted in 1968; production began during 1969 and reached full stride in 1970. At the beginning of 1973 President Nixon suspended Section 235, but production based on previous commitments continued during the year, at a reduced level. Production after 1973 was virtually nonexistent.

There was also a sharp growth in the previously established Section 502 program of the Farmers Home Administration (FHA), which provided a subsidy similar to that of Section 235. New homes in this program tripled from the mid-1960s to 1970, and continued

---

[19] U.S. Bureau of the Census, *Price Index of New One-Family Homes Sold*, series C27.

to increase until 1972. President Nixon suspended the FHA program as well, but production did not decrease as drastically as under Section 235, although 1972 remains the peak year.

The homes built under these programs were far less expensive than the typical new home of the time. In 1970, the average price for a Section 235 home was $16,500, in comparison with $28,600 for all others sold. Buyers under Section 502 bought still less expensive homes. The programs were large enough to distort the new home price distribution in the early 1970s and thus to vitiate the usefulness of those years as the basis of comparisons with later data. In 1970, the first full year of large-scale production, the price of the typical new home sold declined from $25,600 to $23,400—the only year-to-year decline since price statistics were first collected in 1963. When the programs were suspended in 1973, the median new home price rose by 16 percent, the largest increase on record.

It is appropriate to ignore these subsidized homes when analyzing the ability of traditional categories of potential buyers to afford new homes. Both programs were designed for income groups that generally had not bought homes, either new or existing. The typical Section 235 home buyer was in or just above the lowest quarter of the income distribution; today, that home buyer would be eligible for public housing. Middle-income families were not eligible for assistance under either program, and it is unlikely that they would have been interested if they had been eligible. The subsidized homes were small and had few amenities; the average Section 235 home in 1970 had 1,000 square feet, compared to 1,600 square feet for the average non–Section 235 home.[20] During the 1974–1975 recession, middle-income families showed a general lack of interest in the "no-frills" house, which had more frills and was much larger than most Section 235 homes.

The atypical nature of the new home price distribution in 1970 has affected much of the popular discussion of housing affordability. Almost all the national comparisons of housing costs and incomes in the *Time* article began with 1970. So also did recent major analyses by both the Congressional Budget Office and the Joint Center for Urban Studies, which concluded that cost increases have significantly outpaced income increases, creating a new affordability problem.[21]

---

[20] Information on Section 235 homes is taken from U.S. Department of Housing and Urban Development, *1970 Statistical Yearbook*, table 237; that for all new homes sold is taken from U.S. Bureau of the Census, *Characteristics of New One-Family Homes: 1970*, series C25-70-13, 1971, table 42.

[21] U.S. Congress, Congressional Budget Office, *Homeownership: The Changing Relationship of Costs and Incomes, and Possible Federal Roles*, January 1977; and Frieden and Solomon, *Nation's Housing*.

Neither analysis contained any adjustment for the subsidized homes. Had some more typical year been chosen as the base, the trends would be very different; income would rise almost as rapidly as housing prices, both largely in response to inflation.

Trends in Actual Housing Market Behavior

Virtually all of the data and calculations presented so far in this chapter have been based on hypothetical families and rules of thumb. These calculations are no more useful than is the validity of the assumptions underlying them. Until recently, nearly all analyses of housing affordability have been based on such calculations, in large part because there has been very little in the way of data on the housing market behavior of real people. Data on new home purchasers have been available in the decennial census and in occasional special surveys by trade associations, government agencies, or research associations; there has been no consistent, frequent time series.

Fortunately, however, since 1973 data on the characteristics of new and existing home buyers have been collected as part of the Annual Housing Survey (AHS).[22] The AHS sample each year includes a substantial number of new homes, with information on both the characteristics of the unit and the buyer. The survey thus provides hard data on actual housing market behavior. In addition, it is possible to arrange data from the AHS on the same basis as some of the earlier special, infrequent studies; this permits at least some analysis of trends in market behavior, including the perennial question of whether people are finding it harder to buy homes.

Since most of the public concern over housing affordability has been centered on middle-income families, the young, or renters, this discussion will also focus on these groups. Table 5 contains information on the income and age distribution of the actual buyers of new homes, for all years in which consistent information is available. The data cover essentially the past decade and thus are relevant for evaluating the frequently expressed view that middle-income and young families are increasingly being priced out of the market.

Income of New Home Buyers. Contrary to that opinion, the income figures in panel A of table 5 indicate that the income distribution of

---

[22] U.S. Bureau of the Census and U.S. Department of Housing and Urban Development, *Annual Housing Survey*, series H-150. Unless another source is indicated, all data in the remainder of this chapter are taken from the AHS. The published reports usually do not cross-classify the information in enough detail; the author has therefore compiled tabulations from the data tapes.

TABLE 5

INCOME AND AGE OF NEW HOME BUYERS, 1965–1977

Year	Percentage of Buyers in Each Quarter of the Income Distribution				Median Age of Household Head	Percentage of Household Heads Less Than Age 35
	Highest	Second	Third	Lowest		
Panel A						
1965–66	30.4	33.7	24.9	11.1	37.9	39.3
1969	29.9	29.7	26.4	13.9	37.3	NA
1973	21.2	29.8	25.5	23.5	35.1	49.6
1974	30.5	31.3	27.2	15.0	34.9	50.3
1975	30.5	32.9	17.9	19.6	34.9	50.4
1976	30.0	27.9	23.7	18.6	34.0	54.8
1977	32.4	28.1	23.5	16.0	34.3	52.2
Panel B						
1973	26.8	30.7	24.9	17.6	—	—
1974	36.9	32.0	21.4	9.7	—	—
1975	40.5	29.5	18.9	11.1	—	—
1976	34.3	29.5	22.2	14.0	—	—
1977	39.3	27.6	22.4	10.7	—	—

NA = Not available.

SOURCES: Data for 1965–1966 and 1969 are from U.S. Bureau of the Census, *Survey of New Units*. Data for 1965–1966 are published in U.S. Department of Housing and Urban Development, *Housing Surveys*, 1966, part 1: *Occupants of New Housing Units*; 1969 data are from unpublished tabulations. The 1965–1966 sales data are for October 1965 to March 1966; income is for 1965. The 1969 sales and income data are both for the calendar year. Data covering 1973 to 1977 are from U.S. Bureau of the Census and U.S. Department of Housing and Urban Development, *Annual Housing Survey*; calculations by the author are from the data tapes. Sales data are for households moving into new homes from October of the previous year to September of the current year; income is for the current year.

new home buyers has changed very little. Almost exactly 30 percent of new home buyers in each year have been in the upper quarter of the income distribution. The lone exception occurs in 1973, the last year of significant production under the Section 235 program, when the well-to-do families were underrepresented among new home buyers and the lowest income families bought about one-quarter of the homes.

Unfortunately, the income data for 1965–1966 and 1969 include only wages, salaries, and self-employment income; although the Census Bureau collected information on income from other sources, it did not publish a distribution of total income for buyers. For the sake of comparability with the earlier data, the income for the years since 1973 has been restricted correspondingly. This undoubtedly explains the fact that over 10 percent of the buyers have incomes in the lowest quarter. Indeed, for each year since 1973 about 5 percent of all buyers report wage, salary, and self-employment income between zero and $1,000. Most if not all of these buyers are undoubtedly elderly persons living off private pensions, Social Security, and other assets, and probably investing the equity in a former home as the down payment on the new one.[23]

In panel B of table 5, total income has been used to construct a distribution for the five most recent years. As would be expected, the higher income groups are more heavily represented, since these figures include interest and dividends and most home buyers are likely to have some savings; apart from this the figures seem consistent with those in panel A. There is more variability in panel B, but again there is no discernible recent trend.

Importance of Young Buyers. Table 5 also shows the steadily growing importance of young families in the new home market. The median age of household heads declined by over three years, and the proportion of young buyers (those with head of household under 35) increased by over a third. One reason for these results is the demographic change that has occurred as the children of the postwar baby boom have reached maturity and become interested in buying homes; that by itself would tend to bring down the typical age of buyers. But a more important reason is that young families are buying homes, including new ones, to a greater extent than formerly; in each year from 1973 to 1976, between 8 and 10 percent of all young families bought homes in comparison with about 6 percent in 1969–1970 and

---

[23] Frieden and Solomon, in *Nation's Housing*, have compared the 1965–1966 Survey of New Units with a 1975–1976 survey of buyers whose new homes were covered by the Home Owners Warranty program of the National Association of Home Builders (NAHB). They conclude that middle-income families were priced out of the market during the decade. This comparison, however, is invalid, since both the incomes and houses differ between the surveys. As has been mentioned in the text, the published Census Bureau income distributions include only wages, salaries, and self-employment income, while NAHB includes income from all sources. The Census Bureau survey covers all new homes built, while the NAHB survey is restricted almost exclusively to new homes sold; the former category includes homes built on the owner's land, which were between 35 and 40 percent of the total in both the mid-1960s and the mid-1970s. The NAHB survey also reported a significantly lower response rate for buyers of the lowest priced homes, but did not adjust its results for the differential response.

7 percent in 1950–1960. In 1977 the proportion rose to 16 percent. The proportion of young families switching from renting to owning is similarly higher—5 to 7 percent yearly from 1973 to 1976, and 9 percent in 1977, compared with 4¼ percent in 1970.[24] These figures include both new and existing homes; it is unfortunately not possible to separate new and existing homes in the figures before 1973. Between 1973 and 1976, however, between 2¼ and 3 percent of all young families bought new homes each year; the highest figure was recorded in 1976.

Position of Former Renters. The available evidence also suggests that former renters are continuing to buy new homes despite the increases in both prices and interest rates that have been generated by inflation. The proportion of former renters has ranged from 44 percent in 1965–1966 down to 30 percent in 1970, up to 50 percent in 1973, and down to 45 percent in 1974 and 1975, and most recently to 36 percent in both 1976 and 1977.[25] The decline in the mid-1970s probably reflects the importance of equity in an existing home as a means of financing the purchase of a new one, but it is noteworthy that the 1970 figure is still the lowest in the series.

There can be no doubt that inflation has had a deleterious effect on the housing market position of renters. Their plight has attracted attention from politicians and policy makers, and there have been numerous proposals to facilitate home purchases for them; finding new ways to help first-time home buyers is a major policy goal of HUD.[26] Still, many renters have managed to buy homes despite the increasing difficulty. For example, it is clear that rising interest rates and home prices adversely affected renters during the years from 1973 to 1977; but also during those years, some 7.3 million renters became homeowners. This is 30 percent of the 24.7 million households who were renting in 1973. There may be some overstatement in the 7.3 million, since any household can switch tenure in both

---

[24] Data on home buyers in 1959–1960 and 1969–1970 are taken from the decennial censuses of housing: U.S. Bureau of the Census, *1960 Census of Housing,* vol. 4: *Components of Inventory Change,* part 1B: *Inventory Characteristics,* 1962, table 4; and U.S. Bureau of the Census, *1970 Census of Housing,* HC (4)-1, *Components of Inventory Change: United States and Regions,* 1973, table R6. Data on the number of young families are taken from U.S. Bureau of the Census, *Households and Families by Type: March 1976,* Current Population Reports, series P-20, no. 296, 1976, table 3.

[25] This information comes from the same sources as table 5, with the exception that the data for 1970 are taken from U.S. Bureau of the Census, *1970 Components of Inventory Change,* table R4.

[26] "First-Time Buyer to Get HUD Focus, Says Research Chief," *Housing Affairs Letter,* June 29, 1979, p. 1.

directions during the period and could do so more than once; but this phenomenon is unlikely to reduce the overall figures. Over 64 percent of these households (some 4.7 million) were young. The total number of renter households rose during the period by 1.8 million, with about three-quarters of the gross increase in renters consisting of new households, and one-quarter of former renters; thus the extent to which renters have bought homes is not noticeable in the overall data on tenure.

It is interesting and instructive to analyze the market behavior of these first-time home buyers. Few renters can afford to buy the typical new home, according to any conventional rule of thumb, and in fact relatively few renters are buying such homes. They are buying either existing homes or new homes in the lower half of the price distribution. This is particularly true of families in their twenties. It is those families that already own homes that tend to buy the more expensive existing or new homes. Thus, the families that are buying their first homes are putting themselves in a position to move up to a "bigger and better" home a few years into the future rather than switching from renting to owning an expensive new home in a single step.

Moreover, there is little evidence to suggest that these first-time buyers are straining their resources or cutting down on other major purchases to become owners. Most are holding their housing expenditures to within 25 percent of their incomes. Just over half already own two cars before buying a home. This is greater than the proportion of two-car families among all homeowners; so the first-time buyers do not appear to be cutting down on their other major purchases. The homes that these first-time buyers purchase constitute a significant fraction of their assets; their equity is typically about one-third of their net worth (which is usually between $10,000 and $25,000), according to a recent survey by the U.S. League of Savings Associations.[27] Since 63 percent of the first-time buyers in this survey were less than thirty years old, it is perhaps surprising that their equity did not constitute a larger share of their net worth. Despite the difficulty of saving enough for a down payment, few of these first-time buyers were left in the situation of owning a home but nothing else.

While more extensive data—particularly data covering a longer period of time in the past—would be useful, it is hard to see any

---

[27] United States League of Savings Associations, Economics Department, *Homeownership: Realizing the American Dream* (Chicago, Ill.: United States League of Savings Associations, 1978), pp. 44–53.

pattern in the information that is available to indicate that any discernible group in the population is being priced out of the housing market. Instead of having a growing problem, we appear to have a record of steady progress.

7
Policies Designed to Encourage Homeownership

While increased homeownership has been a major goal of federal housing policy for over four decades and programs to achieve this goal have been in existence since the 1930s, policy discussions in recent years have been dominated by the purported increasing difficulty of buying a home, particularly a new one. Several programs have lately been created in response to this problem, and many more have been proposed. The preceding chapter has attempted to show that it is no harder for most households to buy a home now than in the past, and that even those groups supposedly facing the worst problems are buying houses in large numbers; however, it is possible that programs could be developed to make home purchase easier.

This chapter evaluates both the longstanding federal activities to promote homeownership and the newer programs and proposals, which in many cases build on the established ones. Federal policy historically has sought to increase homeownership by lowering the rate of interest on home mortgages or otherwise altering the terms of mortgage contracts. The new programs typically follow in this tradition and operate in mortgage rather than housing markets in the first instance.

FHA Insurance

The federal policy to increase the number of homeowners began during the Great Depression, with the establishment of the Federal Home Loan Bank System (FHLBS) during 1932–1934, and the creation of the Federal Housing Administration (FHA) in 1934.[1] The FHLBS

---

[1] The history of mortgage credit policy, particularly with respect to homeownership, is described in Milton P. Semer et al., "Evolution of Federal Legislative Policy in Housing: Housing Credits," in National Housing Policy Review, *Housing in the Seventies: Working Papers*, 1976, vol. 1, pp. 3–81.

bears a marked resemblance to the Federal Reserve; the twelve regional banks make advances to savings and loan associations when the associations have liquidity problems and otherwise generally fulfill the functions of reserve banks. They are responsible to the Federal Home Loan Bank Board in Washington. Deposit insurance (although savings accounts are not technically deposits) is provided by the Federal Savings and Loan Insurance Corporation, which is similar to the Federal Deposit Insurance Corporation in the case of commercial banks.

In 1938 Congress created the Federal National Mortgage Association (FNMA) as a secondary market facility for FHA-insured mortgages. FNMA had the power to borrow funds in order to buy the mortgages from their originators, on the theory that it could draw funds from areas in which savings were high relative to mortgage demand, and could buy mortgages in areas in which savings were low.

These institutions have served the "conventional" mortgage market. They have had the purpose of increasing the flow of savings into home mortgages; they have usually neither attempted, nor been asked to attempt, to change the practices of lending institutions to achieve social purposes such as broadening homeownership opportunities for low-income families.

The role of innovation was given to FHA. Before the depression the typical home mortgage ran for less than ten years, had a loan-to-value ratio of about 50 percent, and provided for repayment of interest only over the life of the mortgage, with a single "balloon payment" of the entire principal at expiration. FHA encouraged the use of a new type of mortgage: long-term, high loan-to-value ratio (and therefore low down payment), and self-amortizing, with repayment of both principal and interest at a fixed amount each month over the life of the loan. FHA did this by insuring such mortgages, assuming the risk of any loss due to default. Funds to pay the losses on defaulted mortgages came from an insurance premium levied on individual mortgagors. The system was intended to be self-supporting, with the insurance premiums equal to outlays for defaults plus administrative expenses.

Even with the premium (which has usually been 0.5 percent of the outstanding principal balance of the mortgage each year), the longer term of the mortgage brought the monthly payment down to a level at which many more families could be expected to afford it. FHA was intended to increase homeownership among middle-income households in particular. For this purpose, specific dollar limits on the amount of the mortgage were stated in the legislation. The program was known as Section 203, the number of the section of the National Housing Act which established it in 1934.

Success. FHA mortgage insurance was a "social experiment" which has been widely viewed as a success. During the late 1930s over 30 percent of all new homes built had FHA insurance. The proportion of homeowners rose from 44 percent of all households in 1940 to 65 percent in 1976, although the precise contribution of FHA has never been studied. FHA mortgage insurance proved to be actuarially sound: the premiums have more than covered the losses and administrative costs, and the mutual mortgage insurance fund has steadily accumulated reserves which by 1979 totaled about $2.4 billion.[2]

After World War II a parallel program was established by the Veterans Administration (VA), for returning servicemen. The main difference between the two programs is that VA guarantees only a fraction of the loan amount (up to 60 percent, subject to a maximum dollar loss which has been raised from time to time recently to keep pace with inflation). The Veterans Administration program requires no down payment and no mortgage premium and guarantees the loan rather than insuring it, but these differences are minor in comparison with the basic similarities between the programs.

FHA's success was demonstrated in other ways. It showed lenders that long-term self-amortizing mortgages could be profitable, and lending institutions became increasingly more willing to make such loans without FHA insurance against risk, at terms which borrowers found more attractive. During the postwar period FHA accounted for about 15 to 20 percent of new home mortgages annually, which was down from its prewar high.[3]

Decline. FHA also showed that mortgage insurance could be a profitable business. The first private mortgage insurance company began operations in 1957, and by 1970 there were about a dozen such firms. With this increased competition, FHA's market share has declined markedly. The number of FHA-insured new homes declined steadily from 95,000 in 1965 to 23,000 in 1974, before recovering to 43,000 in

---

[2] U.S. Department of Housing and Urban Development, *Budget, U.S. Department of Housing and Urban Development, Fiscal Year 1981*, p. H–28.

[3] U.S. Department of Housing and Urban Development, Office of Policy Development and Research, *Future Role of FHA*, January 18, 1977, p. 10, table 1. Figures on existing home mortgages are less readily available, but the data suggest a similar pattern; see U.S. Department of Housing and Urban Development, *1967 HUD Statistical Yearbook*, p. 75, and *1975 HUD Statistical Yearbook*, pp. 48, 274.

1977. The increase merely parallels the recovery and boom in housing construction, however; FHA activity comprised about 5 percent of the new homes sold in both years. FHA insurance for existing homes has been falling almost as drastically, from 379,000 in 1965 to 106,000 in 1973; it has since risen to 242,000 in 1977.[4] The last figure was about 6.7 percent of all existing homes sold.

While there has been little serious analysis of FHA's decline, a study by David Kaserman concludes that the availability of private mortgage insurance is probably the most important contributing factor.[5] The private insurers have competed effectively with FHA by adapting the VA program approach. They insure only the "top quarter" or some similar fraction of the loans at less cost than FHA charges for insuring the full amount; the lending institution accepts the risk that, in the event of default, it will be unable to sell the home for as much as 75 percent of the outstanding loan balance. Such an eventuality is extremely unlikely for a competent lending institution.

The private mortgage insurers have been able to attract the "better" borrowers in particular from FHA, because of FHA's single-premium structure, under which all borrowers pay the same insurance rate regardless of risk differentials. The cross-subsidization of high-risk mortgagors by lower-risk ones apparently has contributed to the gradual loss of the latter. Thus, the decline of FHA has been manifested both in a lower volume of insurance and in a lower quality of loans for its remaining business. Since 1971 the basic FHA home-ownership program has experienced significant increases in the average loss per claim; its ultimate loss rate is approaching the premium charged, and the program is actuarially sound chiefly because of its past reserve accumulations.

Other explanations for FHA's decline have frequently been offered. During periods of inflation the dollar mortgage limits steadily reduce the potential market for FHA insurance, particularly in more expensive areas. Congress has raised the limits regularly, most recently in 1979. Kaserman's analysis, however, indicates that the limits have had only a minor impact on FHA's market share. The relatively small increase in activity after 1974 provides support for his conclusion.

FHA is also frequently criticized for red tape and processing

[4] U.S. Department of Housing and Urban Development, *1977 HUD Statistical Yearbook*, pp. 60–62, table 5.
[5] David L. Kaserman, "An Econometric Analysis of the Decline in Federal Mortgage Default Insurance," in Robert M. Buckley, John A. Tuccillo, and Kevin E. Villani, eds., *Capital Markets and the Housing Sector: Perspectives on Financial Reform* (Cambridge, Mass.: Ballinger, 1977), pp. 363–79.

delays, particularly in comparison with private mortgage insurers. Both the Ford and Carter administrations have conducted studies of FHA, which called for expedited processing and greater efficiency.[6] While there is no doubt that lengthy processing can be extremely frustrating to both borrowers and lenders, Kaserman's results suggest that this has probably been relatively unimportant. The FHA record can be contrasted with that of VA, which is widely regarded as being more responsive to applicants for its mortgage guarantees and less difficult for lenders and builders to deal with. Since 1965 VA's market share of new home mortgages has remained stable at between 10 and 15 percent while FHA's share has been declining; however, these figures are well below VA's share during the decade immediately after World War II.[7]

Proposals for Revival. As FHA's significance in mortgage lending has declined there have been proposals both to revive it and to define new goals for it. Along the former line, FHA was authorized by Congress in 1974 to coinsure loans on an experimental basis. Under coinsurance the mortgage lender shares in any loss on the loans it originates. It is also responsible for basic underwriting (this differs from the Section 203 program, in which FHA assesses the risk separately—either instead of or in addition to the lender). The elimination of FHA underwriting is expected to reduce processing time on FHA loans. Kaserman views coinsurance as "designed to directly compete with the coverage provided by the private firms in the industry."[8]

Coinsurance has been proposed to meet the concerns of mortgage bankers, who have traditionally been the originators of most FHA and VA loans:[9] the mortgage banking industry has grown with the growth of FHA and VA, and there is some fear within the industry that it might decline with them as well.[10]

To date, the volume of coinsurance has been very small, though it is growing. Some 3,000 loans were coinsured in fiscal year 1979, about as many as in 1977 and 1978 combined. Activity in 1980 and 1981 is expected to decline slightly, however. Nearly all loans were on existing homes. HUD is at present attempting to encourage lenders to make greater use of coinsurance.

---

[6] Department of Housing and Urban Development, *Future Role of FHA,* p. 13; and U.S. Department of Housing and Urban Development, Task Force on the Future of FHA, *Revitalizing the FHA,* n.d. [1977], p. 10.
[7] Department of Housing and Urban Development, *Future of FHA,* p. 10, table 1.
[8] Kaserman, "Decline in Federal Mortgage Default Insurance," p. 378.
[9] Department of Housing and Urban Development, *Future of FHA,* p. 50.
[10] National Housing Policy Review, *Housing in the Seventies,* pp. 71–72.

Much of FHA's remaining business is among relatively low-income home buyers, and there are proposals to expand its activity in this market rather than to seek to compete with private mortgage insurers for middle-income buyers. These proposals often have a geographic or racial focus: FHA should serve central cities or minorities more extensively. The experience with mortgage insurance under the Section 235 program indicates that such mortgagors would probably generate greater risk of default than would the traditional FHA borrower, so that either insurance premiums would need to be raised to achieve actuarial soundness, or explicit subsidies would be required.

Alternative Mortgage Instruments

Another frequent suggestion is that FHA should insure new types of mortgages in addition to the self-amortizing, level-payment fixed-rate mortgage that has become standard. As inflation has increased, many economists and mortgage market analysts have urged the use of alternative mortgage instruments as a means of combating the deleterious effects of the standard mortgage on borrowers or lenders, or both. Some alternative instruments have been used in various parts of the country, but at present they are not widespread. If FHA were to provide insurance for these alternative types they might win market acceptance more quickly. Thus, the successful social experiment of the 1930s might be repeated with new mortgage forms for a new economic situation.

The standard mortgage requires the borrower to pay a constant amount each month. During inflation, lenders insist on higher interest rates to offset the depreciation of the dollars that they receive in repayment of the loan. If the extent of inflation is correctly anticipated, both borrowers and lenders will be in the same position when the loan is repaid that they would be in in a noninflationary environment. The lender will have the same purchasing power and the borrower will have paid the same amount, in real terms. However, the pattern of repayment over the life of the loan will be different. The constant nominal payment is higher because of the inflation. At the beginning of the mortgage, therefore, the borrower's payment is also higher, in real terms; it becomes worth progressively less as the inflation persists for the term of the mortgage. The nominal payments are constant but the real payments decline. With no inflation both nominal and real payments are constant.

Thus, the real payment stream is "tilted" forward, with higher payments in the early years of the mortgage. Home buyers must therefore make higher real payments initially, which may force them to buy a less desirable house than they would in the absence of inflation, or may even price them out of the market altogether.

Graduated Payment Mortgages. One way of alleviating this problem is to adjust the mortgage payment schedule so that nominal payments parallel the inflation rate, rising from a relatively low level at the outset to a level that is above the amount needed to amortize a fixed-payment mortgage of the same principal and term. The payment schedule is established at the time the mortgage is taken out, so that the borrower knows what he or she will have to pay each month. With such a graduated payment mortgage (GPM), the loan is paid off at a lower rate than with a fixed-payment mortgage. This can help the borrower, of course; conversely, it increases the lender's risk exposure because the borrower builds equity in his or her home at a slower rate. It is possible to have a schedule in which payments for the early months or years do not cover the interest; in this instance, the lender's exposure increases and the borrower's equity is reduced.

Graduated payment mortgages have been controversial within the lending community, as might be expected. In 1974 Congress authorized an experimental FHA insurance program for GPMs (Section 245). The regulations promulgated by HUD for this program permitted negative amortization in some cases but required higher down payments than under Section 203, in order that the outstanding principal balance would never be greater during the life of the mortgage than would be permitted for a standard mortgage insured by FHA. Some lenders complained that this approach was too conservative, while others thought it too risky.

Activity under the experimental program was limited; through the end of fiscal year 1977, 471 mortgage commitments were issued by HUD, and 205 loans were insured. However, the insurance volume began to increase after Congress made Section 245 a permanent FHA program in 1977. Some 50,000 graduated payment loans were insured in calendar year 1978 and over 120,000 in 1979. Since late in 1978, graduated payment mortgages have amounted to about one-quarter of FHA's total business.[11]

At most, GPMs may accelerate homeownership, but they do not

---

[11] Information on Section 245 mortgages is taken primarily from U.S. Department of Housing and Urban Development, Office of Housing, Office of Policy and Program Development, *Interim Evaluation of the Graduated Payment Mortgage Program*, December 1979. A description of the experimental program is contained in Chester C. Foster, "The HUD-FHA GPM Experiment," in U.S. Federal Home Loan Bank Board, *Alternative Mortgage Instruments Research Study*, 1977, vol. 1, pp. V–1 to V–48.

appear to open opportunities for families who would otherwise be unable to buy. Section 245 buyers have about the same incomes as those with insurance under Section 203, but the GPM buyers are about a year younger, on average. The houses bought under Section 245 are significantly more expensive and larger. About three-quarters of GPM purchasers are first-time home buyers, which may suggest that the program is increasing homeownership, but the fraction is still larger for Section 203 mortgagors.

The GPM program permits a noticeable reduction in monthly payments during the early years of the mortgage. The range is from 10 to 25 percent for the five types of GPMs insurable. With the 25 percent reduction, payments rise at a rate of 7.5 percent annually and become greater than the standard level-payment mortgage after four years. It is interesting to note that borrowers have overwhelmingly chosen those options with the lowest initial payments. Nearly two-thirds have preferred the plan with the 25 percent reduction in the first year, and another one-fifth have selected the plan with the second greatest reduction (17 percent).

The Homeownership Opportunity Act. Graduated payment mortgages are gaining in popularity politically. In 1979 the National Association of Home Builders (NAHB) proposed an expansion of Section 245 to permit FHA insurance of mortgages on which the outstanding principal balance could exceed the original amount of the loan. Their plan was introduced in Congress as the Homeownership Opportunity Act of 1979 (S.740), with bipartisan support, including that of the chairmen of both the full Senate Banking Committee and its Housing Subcommittee, and the ranking minority member of the subcommittee. Ultimately a modified version was incorporated into the Housing Amendments of 1979.[12]

Both the NAHB proposal and the legislation permitted lower down payments than the original Section 245 had allowed, and the rate of increase in monthly payments was also lower. Thus the outstanding principal balance would quickly rise above the purchase price of the home. The maximum outstanding principal balance was set at 113 percent of the original appraised value.

To be viable, such a plan requires immediate and continuing inflation in home prices; otherwise, the buyer is better off abandoning the home. The necessary appreciation is probably within the long-term trend in home prices and is certainly within recent rates of

---

[12] "House, Senate Conferees Agree on GPM, UDAG Pockets of Poverty Provisions," *Housing and Development Reporter*, December 24, 1979, p. 404.

inflation; therefore, the risk of widespread default and abandonment is probably not great, but the program still could prove to be actuarially unsound.

NAHB has estimated that the program would make homeownership feasible for 8.5 million families, currently priced out of the market, with incomes in the range of $15,000 to $24,000. This figure, however, is a gross overestimate of the probable impact of the program, although it is interesting as an example of the procedures used to calculate affordability, and their limitations. The income range is derived from FHA rules regarding the income required to qualify for insurance, which relate monthly housing expenses (including mortgage payment, taxes, insurance, and other costs) to income. These rules would have required a first-time home buyer making the minimum down payment on a $55,000 house, to have a $28,000 income in the absence of the Homeownership Opportunity Act; under the act, a buyer could qualify with an income of $24,000. The bottom of the income range ($15,000) would have been enough to qualify for a $40,000 mortgage.

Families in this income range are in a much better position in the housing market than is generally recognized. Data from the Annual Housing Survey indicate that, far from being unable to buy a home, most households in this bracket already own one. Slightly over 72 percent were homeowners in 1977—the most recent year for which data are available. Moreover, the incidence of ownership has been increasing—it was less than 67 percent in 1973. (These figures on ownership are for households whose incomes corresponded in real terms to a 1978 income of $15,000 to $24,000; in 1977 the range was about $14,000 to $22,000, for example.)

Families in this real income range were able to buy homes without the aid of GPMs. In 1977 some 9 percent of these families—a total of 2.4 million households—bought a home. While data after 1977 are not yet available, it is likely that this level of home purchase has at least been maintained, since single-family home starts and sales were at or near record levels in both 1978 and 1979, which almost certainly could not have happened if these families had been excluded from the market.

Variable Rate Mortgages. Other types of nonlevel payment mortgages have also attracted attention. Interest has centered on the variable rate mortgage (VRM), in which the interest rate is allowed to change when market rates change. During periods of unanticipated inflation it would rise; during periods of unanticipated deflation it would fall. In the recent past, lenders would clearly have benefited from VRMs, since inflation has largely been unanticipated. In general, VRMs would enable lenders to better match the maturity of their assets and liabilities, since the cost to them of borrowing rises when interest rates rise, but the return on their outstanding mortgage portfolio does not. (Lenders do not face a general increase in the interest cost of all of their liabilities, since Regulation Q limits the interest paid on savings deposits, and will until 1986. However, the six-month money market certificates created in 1978, paying at or above the Treasury borrowing rate, pulled somewhat over half of their funds out of passbook accounts, benefiting savers but creating a further imbalance between the interest rates on lenders' assets and liabilities, and thereby increasing the lenders' desire for VRMs.)[13]

Borrowers benefit to a much smaller extent, if at all, from VRMs. If interest rates rise, then either the monthly payment or the term to maturity must rise. In the former situation borrowers must adjust their household expenditures. From year to year, they cannot know what their mortgage outlay will be. In the event that their incomes do not keep pace with inflation, they may prefer to default on the mortgage rather than devote a continuously increasing share of their income to the mortgage payment. Partly for these reasons, consumer groups have vigorously opposed VRMs, and Congress for several years effectively prohibited federally chartered savings and loan associations from issuing these mortgages. However, state-chartered institutions and commercial banks in California began issuing them in 1975, and mutual savings banks in the Northeast have also issued VRMs. The state-chartered savings associations included the two largest in the country and five of the ten largest (including federally chartered associations). The banks included the Bank of America, the largest bank in the country. In the first year that they were offered, about three-fourths of all home mortgages extended by California savings associations were VRMs. (VRMs are also widely used in Canada and in many European countries, including the United Kingdom and Switzerland.)

Federally chartered savings associations in California felt that they were losing business to the state-chartered institutions and with increasing insistence sought the power to issue VRMs. At the beginning of 1979 the Federal Home Loan Bank Board authorized VRMs in California "to maintain competitive balance."[14] At the same time,

---

[13] "October Is Record Month for Money Market Certificates," *Housing and Development Reporter*, November 27, 1978, p. 659.
[14] "Alternative Mortgage Rules Adopted; VRM Restrictions May Be Put into Law," *Housing and Development Reporter*, December 25, 1978, p. 716.

it permitted GPMs nationally, thus effectively ending the experimental status of the FHA program. Six months later the Federal Home Loan Bank Board authorized VRMs on a national basis as part of a move toward general financial reform advocated by President Carter, despite complaints by several members of Congress, including Congressman Ferdinand St. Germain (D-R.I.), chairman of the Housing Subcommittee in the House.[15] Thus, variable rate mortgages have become generally available, although they cannot be issued by state-chartered institutions in a few states.

VRMs and Homeownership. There has been little opportunity to analyze the effectiveness of VRMs as a means of encouraging home-ownership, but the evidence to date suggests that they will not have a significant impact.

A study of the California experience by Albaum and Kaufman has found that VRM borrowers have had incomes about 10 percent lower than those of conventional borrowers. The minority and ethnic distributions of both types of mortgagors were similar. These results are contrary to the expectations of the consumer groups opposing VRMs. On the other hand, VRM borrowers appear less satisfied with their loans than fixed-rate borrowers are with theirs. Albaum and Kaufman conclude, "This suggests that VRM's are neither as anti-consumer as argued by some critics nor as favorable to consumers as claimed by the lending industry."[16]

The VRMs typically offer some special features to the borrower, including lower prepayment fees, transferability to a later buyer of the home, and in one case, an open line of credit. This may have contributed to the large numbers of VRMs. However, any findings on the desirability of VRMs must be treated with caution at present, as they are still too new.

Variable rate mortgages can increase the opportunities for home-ownership in somewhat the same way that GPMs can, under certain circumstances. If inflation is generally expected to accelerate over the period of the mortgage, lenders will require a higher interest rate on a standard mortgage than on a VRM; the latter can be issued at the current inflation rate (plus the real mortgage interest rate), in the expectation that the rate will rise when inflation does. Thus, home

---

[15] "VRM's, Higher Savings Rates Authorized," *Housing and Development Reporter,* June 11, 1979, p. 25.
[16] Gerald Albaum and George Kaufman, "The Variable Rate Residential Mortgage: Implications for Borrowers," in Federal Home Loan Bank Board, *Alternative Mortgage Instruments Research Study,* vol. 1, pp. VI–1 to VI–47. The quotation is taken from the abstract.

buyers can avert the "tilt" in the real payment stream through a VRM as well as a GPM. But the possibility of unanticipated inflation and the general uncertainty about future interest rates shift much of the risk of higher interest rates from the financial institution to the borrower, who is less well equipped to bear it. There is certainly no reason to prohibit such contracts, however, as Congress has done in the past.

One way to mitigate the exposure of both borrower and lender is through insurance of the risk of interest rate change. This approach was originally suggested by Jack Guttentag and received attention during congressional hearings on financial reform during 1975 and 1976.[17] In effect, the borrower would have a fixed-rate mortgage while the lender would receive payments as if the mortgage were variable; the federal government would assume the risk of interest rate changes. Such an approach has the merit of placing the cost of unanticipated inflation with the government, where the inflation originates, rather than with either the borrower or the lender.

A variety of other alternative mortgage instruments have also received scrutiny. In general, these are designed to meet the concerns of financial institutions confronting inflation rather than those of home buyers and borrowers. They therefore lie outside the scope of this section.[18]

Section 235

FHA has historically sought to bring mortgage interest rates down by removing the risk of default for the lender. Most recent policies and proposals to encourage homeownership have provided for an explicit subsidy of the mortgage rate to bring down monthly housing costs. These proposals take a variety of forms. While all have the

---

[17] Robert Lindsay, "Rate-Risk Insurance for Mortgage Lenders," in U.S. Board of Governors of the Federal Reserve System, *Federal Reserve Staff Study: Ways to Moderate Fluctuations in Housing Construction,* December 1972, pp. 301–22; Robert Edelstein and Jack Guttentag, "Interest Rate Change Insurance and Related Proposals to Meet the Needs of Home Buyers and Home Mortgage Lenders in an Inflationary Environment," in Buckley, Tuccillo, and Villani, eds., *Capital Markets and the Housing Sector,* pp. 191–216; James L. Pierce, "A Program to Protect Mortgage Lenders against Interest Rate Increases," in U.S. Congress, House, Committee on Banking, Currency, and Housing, *Financial Institutions and the Nation's Economy (FINE): A Compendium of Papers Prepared for the FINE Study,* 94th Cong., 1st sess., November 1975, vol. 1, pp. 3–18.

[18] For discussions of the various alternative mortgage instruments, see Donald Lessard and Franco Modigliani, "Inflation and Residential Financing: Problems and Potential Solutions," in Buckley, Tuccillo, and Villani, eds., *Capital Markets and the Housing Sector,* pp. 217–49; and Robert Buckley and John Tuccillo, "An Analysis of Nonlevel Payment Mortgages," in the same work, pp. 271–87.

feature that the interest rate is subsidized, they differ in many ways, such as: whether FHA insurance is available or required; whether the subsidy varies by income; whether the subsidy is restricted to homes of a certain price range, or to new or existing homes; and whether repayment of the subsidy is required when the home is resold.

The deepest subsidy currently available, or proposed, is provided by the Section 235 program. Initially this was designed to promote homeownership for the poor, as described in chapter 2. Buyers were usually in or just above the lowest quarter of the income distribution, with incomes well below those of most home buyers. The homes were small and inexpensive.

In its original form Section 235 was suspended by President Nixon in 1973. However, some $264 million in contract authority remained from congressional appropriations at the time of the suspension. In October 1975 the program was revived, in a modified form, with the release of this $264 million. The funds were expected to provide subsidies for about 250,000 homes.

The revised program differed significantly from the original one in several ways. Most notably, the maximum subsidy was reduced; the buyer had to meet payments on a mortgage with an interest rate of at least 5 percent instead of 1 percent. This of course meant that very low-income families would effectively be excluded from the program, since the minimum mortgage payment that they would have to make from their own income would be $135 per month on a $25,000 mortgage for thirty years. Under the original 1 percent limit, the minimum payment would have been only $81. However, because mortgage interest rates had risen so sharply between 1968 and 1975, the dollar amount of the maximum subsidy was about the same in both the original and the revised program, and the maximum percentage reduction in mortgage payment was about 33 percent in the revised program in comparison with 50 percent initially.

By law, Section 235 is restricted to families with incomes less than 80 percent of the area median. The revised program was thus targeted at families in a narrow income band just below that figure (about $9,000 to $11,000 in 1975 and 1976). There were some new home buyers in this income range—about 80,000 to 100,000 annually from 1973 to 1976; relatively few of them, however (about 20,000 to 30,000), bought homes that would have been eligible for Section 235 under the mortgage limits. It appears that most of these lower-income buyers were trading up—using the equity from an existing home to buy a relatively expensive new one.

Other changes in the program also restricted its market range. Down payment requirements were raised in an attempt to reduce the extent of abandonment and default, and the program was limited to new homes.

There has not been much activity since Section 235 was revived. The record during the first year was termed a disappointment by the Ford administration.[19] HUD projected 10,000 starts during the remainder of fiscal year 1976, but only about 160 actually occurred. Some 18,700 contract reservations were approved for units that builders planned for the program through the end of 1976, but this also was well below the level originally expected.

Several explanations were given for the slow start. As with all FHA programs, mortgage limits for Section 235 are specified in the legislation; they become obsolete in periods of inflation. The limits were raised during 1976 and 1977 for the third and fourth times since the program was created. The down payment requirements were reduced in 1976, and the maximum subsidy was increased in 1977; a family can now pay off its mortgage at a rate as low as 4 percent. These changes, however, apparently have not had a major impact; production through September 1979 totaled less than 20,000 units compared to a HUD projection of 100,000.

More fundamental problems have also been suggested. The complaint of FHA processing delays applies to Section 235 as well as to the traditional mortgage insurance programs; many builders do not like to deal with FHA. The program also suffers from inconsistencies in the restrictions placed on eligibility for buyers and homes. The income limits vary by metropolitan area, but the mortgage amount is fixed, with variation permitted only between "high" and "low" cost areas, and then only by a factor of 17 percent. Since median incomes have much greater dispersion than 17 percent across the country, the statute causes the mortgage limits to be too low in relation to the maximum income eligibility in some areas and too high in others. It is always possible for builders to construct homes within the mortgage limits, but, again, this is more difficult in inflationary periods when costs are rising. The income limits create a "notch" effect: families earning 80 percent of the area median can receive a subsidy of perhaps $600 annually; families earning 81 percent can receive nothing.

These problems could be ameliorated by changes in the legislation. Greater regional variability in mortgage limits, or less in income, would be desirable; and raising the income ceiling to the area median or removing it entirely would eliminate the "notch" and extend the

[19] U.S. Office of the President, *Ninth Annual Report on the National Housing Goal*, 95th Cong., 1st sess., January 1977, p. 6.

program to a greater number of families. Since a buyer must pay at least 20 percent of his or her income toward the mortgage, including taxes and insurance, the program would still be effectively restricted to families at or below the median income, even if there were no explicit income limit.

Section 235 has been trying to reach an income group that has not been participating in the new home market to any sizable extent. To date, it has not succeeded. However, the approach embodied in the program has attracted attention as a means of assisting "middle-income" families and stimulating the home-building industry. In mid-1980, the Carter administration proposed to convert most of the unobligated Section 235 budget authority to such a middle-income subsidy by raising the sales price limit to $60,000, and either eliminating the income limit altogether or raising it to 120 percent of the area median (about $24,000 nationally). If this program were approved by Congress, it would leave funds for only about 18,000 homes in the lower-income "revised" program, in addition to the 50,000 approved so far.

The administration's proposal stems from concern about output and employment in home building, at least as much as from the sense that "middle-income" families, however defined, are being priced out of the market for homes. Given these goals, an income-related subsidy such as Section 235 might be the least expensive means of achieving them. Since the subsidy falls as income rises, young upwardly mobile families could be assisted at fairly low cost over a short period of years until their incomes increased to the point where they were no longer entitled to assistance. This has in fact been happening in the original Section 235 program. By mid-1979, some 35 percent of the households originally subsidized were no longer receiving assistance, because of their increased incomes. Less than 25 percent were still being subsidized, and the average subsidy was about $50 per month, down from about $80 in 1972. The remaining 40 percent of the subsidized households was about equally divided between those who had defaulted on the mortgage and those who had prepaid it.

The Tandem Plan

A different form of interest rate subsidy was used extensively during the 1974–1975 housing recession as a countercyclical device to stimulate housing production, and is being actively considered in 1980; its history illustrates the difficulty of increasing homeownership by such a means. The program, known as the Tandem Plan, began in the summer of 1971 in response to political concern that rising interest

124

rates would abort the housing recovery then under way, but the plan has been used much more extensively since it was reimplemented in 1974.[20] Under the Tandem Plan the Government National Mortgage Association (GNMA) offers to purchase mortgages that have interest rates below the market rate. GNMA buys these mortgages at par from the private lenders originating them. In turn, GNMA either sells them to private investors or uses them as backing for pass-through securities, guaranteeing to pay the security buyer the monthly principal and interest due from the home buyer. The resale occurs at the price the market will bear. Since the mortgages pay a below-market interest rate they can only be sold to private investors at a discount from their face value. The discount constitutes the subsidy; it is absorbed by GNMA and is financed by congressional appropriations.

The form of the subsidy thus differs from that of Section 235 in that its present value over the entire life of the mortgage is paid by the government at about the time the home is purchased. This is appropriate in view of the plan's purpose of mitigating housing production recessions; the full subsidy is provided when the stimulus is most desired.

Tandem was originally restricted to FHA or VA mortgages, but since 1974 it has been available for conventional mortgages as well. It has been used to stimulate both single-family and multifamily production, depending on which sector has seemed weakest. Between 1974 and 1976, GNMA made commitments to purchase about $18 billion of mortgages, covering about 700,000 homes and apartments. The amount of the subsidy is of course much less, but it has been increasing. In 1974 and through the first half of 1975 the maximum contract interest rate was 7.75 percent, while in mid-1975 it was cut to 7.50 percent. During the period, market interest rates were fairly stable. The subsidy to the home buyer is proportional to the difference between the market and the contract interest rate. The cost to the federal government can vary, since the mortgages are sold at a much later time than they are originated, and market rates may have risen or fallen in the interim.

The Tandem Plan has been very popular among home builders, who regard it as particularly desirable in periods of disintermediation, when savers are withdrawing funds from conventional mortgage lenders. Changes in the mortgage market since 1976, however, are likely to limit its usefulness, if not eliminate the need for it altogether.

---

[20] A description of the Tandem Plan is provided in Ronald Utt, "An Empirical Analysis of the GNMA Tandem Plan," in Buckley, Tuccillo, and Villani, eds., *Capital Markets and the Housing Sector*, pp. 347–62; see especially pp. 347–48.

The creation of money market certificates has apparently reduced the cyclical sensitivity of savings and loan deposits, so that they have more funds available now when interest rates rise. Savings and loan associations also are a less important source of mortgage finance generally than they used to be; insurance companies and pension funds have been more active in recent years.

Academic research on the plan's effectiveness has yielded mixed results. Hendershott and Villani have concluded that mortgage purchases by GNMA, including Tandem mortgages, help to smooth out housing cycles by lowering interest rates at the time of the program but do not generate much, if any, permanent increase in the stock of housing; with Tandem, production is lower in the later periods than it would be if Tandem were not used during the housing recession.[21] Such an outcome is precisely what the plan was originally intended to achieve.

A contrary result has been reported by Ronald Utt, who found no significant impact of Tandem Plan commitments (lagged one quarter) on housing starts. This occurred because Tandem generated a decline in the supply of new housing—a result which, Utt notes, is "at variance with virtually all other econometric investigations of federal mortgage credit support."[22] Utt's research, however, is the only econometric study focusing exclusively on the Tandem Plan.

George von Furstenberg has calculated the savings to home buyers from Tandem financing, estimating that total savings amount to about $700 million, or 6.5 percent of the face value of the mortgages purchased.[23] He assumes, however, that Tandem does not affect the housing market in any significant way but simply provides below-market financing for buyers who would nearly all buy homes without it. Von Furstenberg's analysis and calculations have subsequently been challenged by Robert Buckley, who relies on several econometric analyses of the mortgage market to argue that benefits to mortgagors are much larger, and the countercyclical effect is greater, because the GNMA purchases largely represent increases in the available supply of mortgage funds, and thus drive down the interest rate for all home buyers in the short run.[24]

---

[21] Patric H. Hendershott and Kevin E. Villani, "The Federally Sponsored Credit Agencies: Their Behavior and Impact," in Buckley, Tuccillo, and Villani, eds., *Capital Markets and the Housing Sector*, pp. 291–309.

[22] Utt, "Empirical Analysis of the GNMA Tandem Plan," p. 354.

[23] George von Furstenberg, "Distribution Effects on GNMA Home Mortgage Purchases and Commitments under the Tandem Plan," *Journal of Money, Credit, and Banking*, vol. 8 (August 1976), pp. 373–89.

[24] Robert M. Buckley, "Comment," *Journal of Money, Credit, and Banking*, vol. 10 (August 1978), pp. 379–83.

While the findings of these studies differ, none of them indicate that Tandem has been especially successful in increasing homeownership. Neither Hendershott and Villani nor Buckley report a substantial increase in housing production over the cycle. Buckley's calculations suggest that perhaps 3 percent of the homes built would not have been sold—a total of about 50,000 over the two years from mid-1974 to mid-1976. If the analysis of Hendershott and Villani is correct, the program has been effective in mitigating the severity of the business cycle in housing construction, but it has done so by changing the time pattern of production over the cycle, not by increasing production overall.

Studies of the buyers' side of the market suggest a similar conclusion. A comparison of Tandem and unsubsidized borrowers by the Congressional Research Service of the Library of Congress concluded that there was little difference in the incomes of the two groups but that Tandem buyers bought more expensive homes.[25] This study also found that about 9 percent of the Tandem-assisted borrowers had incomes of $30,000 or more, which generated political concern over the distributional effects of the program. There are mortgage limits in the Tandem Plan, as in nearly all government housing programs, but not income limits on borrowers.

Since 1976 Tandem has been used primarily for apartment projects, as production of single-family homes has increased. The Carter administration has transformed it into a program for subsidized housing, offering Tandem loans for Section 8 projects. The administration has also created a "targeted Tandem Plan" for projects in central cities. Tandem has not so far been used explicitly to increase homeownership, although the concern over the incomes of Tandem buyers suggests that Congress may revive it in this more restricted way, perhaps during the present (1980) cyclical downturn. The goal of broadening homeownership is likely to prove at least partially incompatible with that of moderating construction cycles: the narrower the segment of the population eligible for Tandem, the longer it will take to achieve a given number of assisted housing starts, and thus the smaller the countercyclical impact will be. However, Tandem is directed at subsidizing interest rates, which are the relevant component of housing costs to subsidize in order to mitigate the effects of inflation on potential home buyers.

---

[25] Grace Milgram et al., *The Effect of the Brooke-Cranston Program: A Comparison of Assisted and Unassisted Home Mortgages in 1975* (Washington, D.C.: Library of Congress, Congressional Research Service, September 22, 1976); see especially pp. 39–46.

Local Mortgage Revenue Bonds

In 1978 a new way of lowering mortgage interest rates was developed, which spread rapidly but also aroused substantial opposition. This was the local mortgage revenue bond, a device intended to secure for home buyers the cost savings that local governments achieve from the tax exemption enjoyed by their bonds.

The program works in the following way. A municipality issues tax-exempt long-term bonds. The proceeds of the bond sale are used to finance home mortgages, which are originated and serviced by local savings and loan associations or other thrift institutions. A commercial bank working with the program makes interest and principal payments to bondholders, using funds generated from the mortgage payments made by the home buyers. The sponsoring municipality has no involvement in the operation of the program; it merely lends its authority to issue tax-exempt bonds and establishes guidelines regarding mortgagors who may benefit from the program.[26] The early plans offered mortgage interest rate reductions of about two full percentage points, from 10 to 8 percent. This represents a savings of some $85 per month in interest payments on a $60,000 loan; it is slightly larger than the savings realized by Tandem Plan mortgagors.

The first bonds were issued by Chicago in July 1978 in the amount of $100 million. Denver quickly followed with an issue of $50 million, and by the end of April 1979 about $1.6 billion had been issued. This rapid growth rate was expected to continue, but at that point Congress began considering legislation to limit the bonds to low- and moderate-income households, with a clause making the limitation retroactive to the date the bill was issued (April 25). The retroactivity clause effectively halted the issuance of mortgage revenue bonds, while municipalities, bond buyers, and underwriters waited to see if the bill would pass. This bill (H.R. 3712) embodied the position of the Carter administration and had bipartisan support from senior members of the House Ways and Means Committee, but many members of Congress were concerned about the apparently increasing difficulty of buying a home, and favored either the bonds or some other form of subsidy instead. The legislative course of the bill was complex, and in August 1979 the moratorium on bond issues was partially lifted, as it became clear that Congress was having difficulty

---

[26] Unless otherwise indicated, the information in this section is taken from John A. Tuccillo and John C. Weicher, *Local Mortgage Revenue Bonds: Economic and Financial Impacts* (Washington, D.C.: The Urban Institute, 1979).

agreeing on a bill. An additional $1.4 billion worth of bonds was issued by the end of the year, after the moratorium was lifted.[27]

In March 1980, nearly a year after the original bill was introduced, the House passed a compromise measure (H.R. 5712) prohibiting mortgage revenue bonds after two years from the date of passage, and in the meantime limiting the buyer's income to 115 percent of the area median, which in general would be substantially below the ceilings typical of the original programs.[28] At this writing, the Senate has not begun consideration of the bill, and its chances of enactment appear problematical.

The opposition to the bonds comes largely from those concerned about the revenue lost to the Treasury. Mortgage revenue bonds reduce the taxes paid to the federal government, to the extent that they displace conventional lending. Advocates have claimed that the forgone tax revenue is well "spent" because the bonds increase home-ownership.

E. F. Hutton, the brokerage house that created the concept and underwrote the Chicago bonds, has asserted that they help to provide "affordable housing for the largely forgotten moderate- and middle-income class—the family earning from $14,000 to $25,000 annually, which today finds it difficult, if not impossible, to purchase a home."[29] This may sound familiar; it is almost exactly the same income range for which the National Association of Home Builders' Homeowner-ship Opportunity Act was intended. Perhaps it is worth repeating that most households in this class already own homes, and a substantial number have been buying each year, without the benefit of mortgage revenue bonds or graduated payment mortgages.

In practice, the mortgage revenue bonds have apparently not broadened the opportunities for homeownership. In Chicago the income distribution of households assisted by the bonds was almost identical with that of conventionally financed buyers. The median incomes were $19,900 and $19,600, respectively, indicating that if anything the assisted buyer was slightly better off. Chicago had an income limit of $40,000 for its program, which excludes only about 10 percent of Chicago home buyers. Other programs have had similar,

[27] George E. Peterson, John A. Tuccillo, and John C. Weicher, "The Impact of Local Mortgage Revenue Bonds on Securities Markets and Housing Policy Objectives," paper presented at the Conference on Efficiency in the Municipal Bond Market, Portland, Oregon, January 1980.

[28] "House Passes Mortgage Revenue Bond Bill," *Housing and Development Reporter*, March 31, 1980, p. 913.

[29] "E. F. Hutton Talks about Forgotten American Families," advertisement by E. F. Hutton & Company, Inc., *Washington Post*, April 4, 1979, p. D12.

though usually lower, limits. The typical ceiling of $30,000 excluded only about a quarter of all home buyers.

Direct Lending

There have frequently been proposals, analogous to the local mortgage revenue bond, to lower interest rates by having the federal government make mortgage loans directly. Since the Treasury is able to borrow at lower interest rates than other financial institutions, including private mortgage lenders, it would be possible for the Treasury to borrow and lend to home buyers at lower interest rates than could a savings association, and no budgetary appropriation would be required.

These proposals sometimes involve channeling the loans through the Federal Financing Bank, an agency of the Treasury established by Congress in 1973 to coordinate the capital borrowing of other federal agencies by issuing its own securities in lieu of theirs. More recently, this bank has become a conduit through which funds borrowed by the Treasury (rather than the bank in its own name) are lent to the agencies.

Such proposals implicitly assume that the Treasury will be able to increase its borrowing without driving up either the interest it must pay on its debt or interest rates generally. Several economic analyses of Treasury borrowing have concluded that this outcome is unlikely. Two of the more detailed studies suggest that the effect of an additional $1 billion of Treasury borrowing would be to raise the short-term borrowing rate by about 0.8 to 0.9 percent, or just under one hundred basis points. This effect would be dissipated after a few years and interest rates would return to their initial levels, but the Treasury would incur higher costs during the period of adjustment.[30] A joint study by the Treasury and HUD of two subsidized production programs (Section 236 and Section 802) concluded that the indirect effect of increased Treasury borrowing costs would approximately offset the direct savings to home buyers.[31] Furthermore, interest rates for all mortgagors would be driven up by the Treasury borrowing as

---

[30] Hendershott and Villani, "The Federally Sponsored Credit Agencies"; Barry Bosworth and James S. Duesenberry, "A Flow of Funds Model and Its Implications," in Federal Reserve Bank of Boston, *Issues in Federal Debt Management* (Boston, Mass.: Federal Reserve Bank of Boston, 1973), pp. 39–149.

[31] "Report by the Secretary of the Treasury and the Secretary of Housing and Urban Development on the Financing of Programs Authorized under Section 236 of the National Housing Act and Section 802 of the Housing and Community Development Act of 1974," n.d. [October 1975], appendix B, p. 9.

funds were withdrawn from savings institutions; again, this would be a temporary phenomenon.

The net effect would thus be to subsidize some home buyers at the expense of the taxpayers and other buyers. The scheme would not be without cost to the federal government or to the taxpayers. It would also undoubtedly require administrative judgments as to which buyers should receive the subsidy and thus would introduce further political distortions into the housing market.

Section 202. At present there are two direct lending housing programs: Section 202, which is available to nonprofit (usually religious) sponsors of apartment projects for the elderly, and the Farmers Home Administration's Section 502, which makes low-interest loans to low-income home buyers in rural areas in a manner similar to that of the original Section 235 program.

Section 202 has been in existence since 1959. At first the federal government lent to the sponsor at its own borrowing rate plus administrative costs of 0.5 percent. In 1964 this procedure was changed, and the rate was set at 3 percent regardless of federal borrowing costs. Under either arrangement, however, the subsidy was not deep enough to enable low-income elderly couples or individuals to live in the projects unless they received additional subsidies. In 1968, therefore, HUD began to combine Section 202 with the newly enacted Section 236, under which interest rates could be subsidized down to as low as 1 percent. After 1968 most Section 202 projects also included the Section 236 subsidy. The program was suspended in 1973, but was reactivated in the 1974 Housing and Community Development Act with the original interest rate provision. Federal borrowing rates had of course risen substantially since 1964, and so the revised program could not bring new housing within the financial reach of low-income households; it was therefore combined with the new Section 8 program.

Until fiscal year 1979, the program was traditionally off-budget. The funds borrowed by the Treasury to lend to the sponsors did not appear in the federal deficit. This contributed to the popularity of the program but did not affect its economic impact—including the extent to which it drives up all Treasury borrowing rates.

Section 202 has been a relatively small program. About 14,000 apartments were built under the original program from 1959 to 1965. With the deeper subsidy available under the fixed borrowing rate, some 20,000 more were started during the next three years. From 1969 through 1976 an additional 52,000 were started, of which 38,000 included the Section 236 subsidy. Through fiscal year 1979, 50,000 had been started under the 1974 program. Although less than 150,000 apartments have been built, the program is immensely popular politically: President Carter expressed support for it during the first of his televised campaign debates with President Ford.

Drawbacks. The record of Section 202 makes it clear that direct federal mortgage lending provides relatively small interest rate savings unless it is accompanied by some other subsidy. For middle-income buyers who are supposedly priced out of the market, such a subsidy might be sufficient inducement to buy. The subsidies that would be available at current Treasury borrowing rates, however, are lower than those offered by the Tandem Plan, and the qualitative impact of borrowing to finance either form of subsidy would be the same. There is thus no particular reason, from the home buyer's standpoint, for favoring direct federal mortgage lending, and there are several reasons for preferring Tandem—for example, making explicit the nature of the subsidies provided by the federal government, and minimizing the number of federal programs which attempt to achieve the same purpose with very nearly the same mechanism.[32]

Deferred Interest Payments

The history of Section 202 and the continued interest in direct lending illustrate the political popularity of programs which require no explicit appropriation and thus appear to be costless to the federal government. The absence of budget outlays has been an important attribute of several other proposals, some of them ingenious, designed to increase homeownership without spending money. In 1976, for example, then Senator William Brock (R-Tenn.) and Congressman Thomas L. Ashley (D-Ohio) introduced the Housing Incentive Investment Act (S. 3193). Under this legislation home buyers would pay an interest rate on their mortgage that was 2 percent below the market rate. The other 2 percent would be paid by the Government National Mortgage Association, with funds borrowed from the Treasury. Whenever the homeowner sold his or her house, he or she would repay the accumulated subsidy with interest to GNMA.

The Brock-Ashley bill recognized the difficulty created by higher interest rates in periods of inflation and also recognized the fact that inflation was driving up home prices. It attempted to combine the

---

[32] An example of proposals of this type is H.R. 1081, "The Home Owners Mortgage Loan Corporation Act," introduced by Congresswoman Leonor Kretzer Sullivan (D–Mo.) and Congressman William A. Barrett (D–Pa.) in the 94th Cong., 1st sess., January 1975.

two effects of inflation into one package that would facilitate home-ownership without adding to the federal deficit. Whether the bill would have had such an effect is problematical. The subsidy would lower monthly payments by almost 10 percent, but it would also lower the rate of equity buildup for the buyer. After fifteen years, for example, the Brock-Ashley mortgagor with a twenty-five year mortgage would owe the lender and GNMA combined about 15 percent more than the original debt, whereas, if the buyer had a conventional mortgage, there would be a reduction of 34 percent. The difference in equity appreciation is thus about 50 percent of the original principal amount of the mortgage. It is questionable whether buyers would be interested in such a trade-off between earlier homeownership and a lower payment on the one hand, and a lower rate of return on their investment on the other. In view of the rates of price appreciation and return on other investments of the past decade, the typical Brock-Ashley buyer would probably profit more from home purchase than from alternative investments such as savings accounts, but by much less than with a conventional, unsubsidized mortgage.

The subsidy repayment provisions could create additional problems for the federal government. If the value of the home does not increase by enough to enable the owner to repay the subsidy, the owner's best economic option is simply to abandon the home when he or she decides to move rather than to try to sell it. This of course would leave the government with a loss and with a home that it would then have to resell, raze, or otherwise dispose of. On the basis of the patterns of the past decade, it appears that the typical subsidy recipient would in fact probably be able to repay the accumulated subsidy upon resale; but it is likely that the federal government would still acquire some homes which did not appreciate rapidly enough and would then incur the same difficulties that have arisen under the original Section 235 program, as described in chapter 3.

The Brock-Ashley bill would "work" only in a period of continued inflation. With a slowing of the rate of price increase to the average level of the past twenty-five years, for example, the typical participant would just barely be able to repay the accumulated subsidy on resale. Stated another way, about half of all subsidized home buyers would find it profitable to default and abandon their homes.

As introduced, the bill also contained a provision that all subsidized mortgages would have variable interest rates; in periods of unanticipated inflation buyers would find their obligation to GNMA increasing. If mortgage rates rose by 2 percent the GNMA monthly payment to the lender, and lien on the house, would double. The buyer could correspondingly expect an increase in the value of his home, however, which would enable him or her to repay the additional subsidy on resale.

The subsidy and variable rate provisions were combined in the bill in an apparent attempt to appeal to both borrowers and lenders and thus increase the chances of passing the bill. The Brock-Ashley variable rate provision was something like the interest rate risk insurance approach described earlier in that borrowers would pay at a fixed rate while lenders would receive interest at a variable rate. There was a crucial difference between the two proposals, however: the Brock-Ashley bill made the homeowner ultimately liable for the difference in interest costs, at the time of resale. It thus compounded the negative effect of the interest rate subsidy on the owner's rate of equity accumulation and placed the burden of unanticipated inflation and interest rate changes on the person least able to bear the risk.

Despite its intent, it is not clear that the Brock-Ashley bill would in fact have increased homeownership. The bill was limited to mortgages of $35,000 or less, which would perhaps have implied a typical home price of between $40,000 and $45,000. Even at the lower price a large number of homes then being sold would have qualified for assistance: about 40 percent of new homes and 50 percent of existing ones had prices below $40,000 in 1976. A large number of families buying either new or existing homes could thus have availed themselves of the subsidy. To the extent that they did so, the bill would have subsidized them to do what they already planned to do, rather than enhancing homeownership. (Congressman Ashley favored restricting the bill to new homes only, while Senator Brock wished to include existing homes as well.[33] The restriction, as Congressman Ashley recognized, would have substantially reduced any possible effectiveness in encouraging homeownership and would have greatly reduced the appeal of the variable rate provision from the lender's standpoint.)

Down Payment Subsidies

Most proposals intended to increase homeownership have provided some kind of interest rate subsidy, but political attention has lately been focused on the possibility of reducing the difficulty of accumulating a down payment. In 1976 and 1977 Senator Edward Brooke

---

[33] U.S. Congress, Senate, Committee on Banking, Housing, and Urban Affairs, *Development of New Types of Mortgage Instruments*, 94th Cong., 2nd sess., August 4, August 9, and August 10, 1976. Senator Brock's statement appears on p. 12 and Congressman Ashley's on pp. 58–60.

134

(R-Mass.) introduced the Young Families' Housing Act, which would permit families to establish tax-sheltered Individual Housing Accounts (IHAs) similar to the Individual Retirement Accounts now in existence. Both principal and interest in an IHA would be exempt from federal income taxation. The IHA was intended to be limited to current renters and thus was intended to stimulate ownership rather than new home production, but the bill as introduced did not include such a restriction.[34] Despite its title, the legislation did not limit the age for IHA holders.

The rationale for this kind of subsidy is the argument that home prices are high and are rising rapidly, and that they constitute the major impediment to home purchase. The evidence discussed in the previous chapter does not support this contention. Prices of new homes are not rising much more rapidly than incomes; the contrary impression has arisen because of the relatively large share of small, subsidized homes for low-income families during the early 1970s. Instead, home prices and incomes have increased in almost exactly the same ratio.

Similarly, down payments as a share of purchase price have remained nearly constant during the 1970s. Conventional loans have typically had a down payment of about 25 percent according to the Federal Home Loan Bank Board.[35] The bank board data actually indicate a very slight decline in down payment ratios since the early 1960s. Down payments on new homes sold have also been stable at around 15 percent for conventional loans.[36] Much lower down payments have been available through the federal housing programs. FHA buyers may put as little as 3 percent down on a $25,000 home, and the typical FHA down payment is about 5 percent. The 3 percent rule also applies to the first $25,000 of the mortgage on a higher priced home. The requirements have been lowered by Congress on several occasions, most recently in 1969; before that date the minimum down payment applied to the first $20,000 of the mortgage. The Veterans Administration guarantees mortgages with no down payments and the typical VA mortgage is, and has been, in this category. The same is true of the subsidized Farmers Home Administration programs.

---

[34] The two proposals were S. 3692, introduced in the 94th Congress in 1976, and S. 664, introduced in the 95th Congress in 1977. These two versions of the Young Families' Housing Act differed in some provisions, but both provided for Individual Housing Accounts.

[35] *Federal Home Loan Bank Board Journal*, vol. 10, no. 1 (January 1977), S. 5. 1, p. 40.

[36] U.S. Bureau of the Census and U.S. Department of Housing and Urban Development, *Characteristics of New Housing*, Construction Reports, C25–75–13, pp. 48–49, table 19. Various differences in coverage between the bank board and Census Bureau data account for the difference in the down payment ratios.

The effectiveness of the IHA in increasing homeownership is thus open to question. It would certainly shorten the period of time that families would require in order to save up for a down payment of any particular amount. This would occur both because the return on the amounts initially saved would be greater and because these families would be encouraged to save a higher proportion of their income. The IHA would thus accelerate the process of becoming homeowners for those families intending to buy and would increase the rate of homeownership during that period. Whether it would cause families to decide to buy rather than rent over their full life-cycle is more problematical. The plan does not greatly reduce the cost of buying rather than renting. If we assume a 15 percent down payment and a 25 percent marginal tax bracket for the typical renter, the cost of a new home would be reduced by less than 4 percent ($0.15 \times 0.25 = 0.0375$). Some further cost saving could occur as families choose to make larger down payments, but this effect would probably be relatively small. There has been very little serious analysis of the responsiveness of the tenure choice decision to the relative costs of owning and renting, but it would have to be rather high for the IHA to increase homeownership to any noticeable extent.

Program Cost. Regardless of the program's effectiveness, the cost of the IHA would be high because many households already switch tenure each year and would be eligible for the program. Published estimates of the cost have varied widely. The cost depends on the number of eligible households, the participation rate, the maximum tax deduction, and the proportion of the deduction actually taken. Kenneth Rosen, who originally developed the IHA, has testified that it would cost about $6 billion, with 2.5 million households participating, over a ten-year period.[37] Computations prepared by HUD in response to Rosen's testimony indicated that between 19.0 and 22.7 million households could be expected to buy their first homes over the decade 1975–1985 and would thus be eligible for the subsidy; with the same tax loss figure per account, the forgone revenue would be $45–55 billion over that decade.[38]

Rosen has also proposed a modified version of the IHA with an income limit of $20,000 for eligibility. This would reduce the cost of

[37] Kenneth T. Rosen, "Statement on S. 664," in U.S. Congress, Senate, Committee on Banking, Housing, and Urban Affairs, *Young Families' Housing Act of 1977: Hearings,* 95th Cong., 1st sess., March 31 and April 1, 1977, p. 38.

[38] U.S. Department of Housing and Urban Development, "An Estimate of the Tax Loss Generated by the Individual Housing Account (IHA) Proposal (S. 664)," in Senate Banking Committee, *Young Families' Housing Act: Hearings,* p. 291.

the program somewhat, but 70 percent of first-time home buyers in the period 1973–1976 had incomes of less than $20,000 (adjusted for inflation for years before 1976). For this program, also, cost estimates vary. Rosen calculates that "first-year costs would be about $600 million, and steady-state costs would be about $1–2 billion."[39] He bases the calculations on a similar Canadian program, begun in 1974, and multiplies the number of Canadian participants by the ratio of U.S. to Canadian housing starts to obtain an estimate of 1 million participants each year. (The IHA, however, applies to existing homes as well as new ones.)

On the basis of actual sales of new and existing homes in the United States over the past five years and the proportion of first-time buyers among all home purchasers, Buckley estimates that about 1.85 million households would be eligible to participate in the program each year. He calculates the forgone revenue as about $3 billion per year,[40] about two-thirds of the forgone tax revenues from the mortgage interest deduction on the federal income tax. This appears more reasonable than Rosen's estimates.

These revenue losses are loosely the cost of subsidizing those first-time buyers who purchase homes in the absence of any subsidy. The cost will be greater to the extent that other renters are induced to become buyers or that the process of saving for a down payment is accelerated by the program. In these situations, the program costs should be measured against the number of additional buyers generated by the plan; this number would have to be very large to bring the cost per incremental buyer down to a figure comparable with current subsidy programs. If there were 200,000 additional buyers annually, for example, the cost per incremental buyer, using Buckley's assumptions, would be about $12,000. This is about $5,000 more than the cost of the original Section 235 low-income homeownership program.[41]

Tax Credit. While there is at present little direct evidence on the possible effectiveness of such a program in increasing homeownership, recent experience with the federal income tax credit for new

[39] Kenneth T. Rosen, "The Housing Crisis and the Homeownership Incentive Plan," *AREUEA Journal*, vol. 5 (Fall 1977), pp. 366–79; see especially pp. 376–78.
[40] Robert M. Buckley, "On Estimating the Tax Loss of the Homeownership Incentive Plan," *AREUEA Journal*, vol. 6 (Spring 1978), pp. 106–10.
[41] These calculations are based on data for Section 235 on program "run-out" costs and the number of participating families as of 1972, taken from National Housing Policy Review, *Housing in the Seventies*, pp. 95 and 106. The costs are then inflated by the increase in the consumer price index since 1972, so that the programs can be compared at a given time.

home purchases suggests that the effectiveness would be minimal. In 1975 Congress enacted a credit for 5 percent of the purchase price of a new home, up to $2,000, for homes started before March 29, 1975 (the date the bill became law), and purchased before the end of the calendar year.[42] The tax credit is essentially a deferred down payment subsidy; the $2,000 is about the average of the two estimates of tax savings per home buyer through the IHA that have been presented by Rosen. Thus, the credit can serve as at least a rough approximation to the IHA despite the differences in the timing of the subsidy.

The impact of the tax credit was subsequently evaluated by both the Federal Home Loan Bank Board and HUD. Neither found that it stimulated sales to any appreciable extent. The HUD study was especially detailed, analyzing the sales of new homes on the basis of the month in which the home was started. It found virtually no change in the sales pattern from 1975 to 1976, except for a very slight upturn in the sales of eligible homes in April, the first month in which the credit was available. The study estimated that the tax credit had generated incremental sales of about 4,000 homes during its first seven months, out of a total of 309,000 sold.[43] Since 157,000 of the new homes sold—just over half the total—were eligible for the credit, the HUD study results imply that the tax revenue loss would amount to over $78,000 per eligible new home sold as a result of the credit, if all buyers of eligible homes were to claim the full amount.

The Tax Treatment of Homeowners

The oldest mechanism for stimulating homeownership is the treatment for purposes of income taxation of the expenses incurred and income received by homeowners. Many of the provisions specifically affecting housing have been part of the income tax law since the earliest days of the tax; some even go back to the income tax enacted during the Civil War. Thus, the tax treatment of homeowners originally was not specifically a policy to encourage ownership. Gradually, however, it has come to be regarded in this light by both policy makers and analysts. Some parts of the tax law have been modified

---

[42] P. L. 94–12, Sec. 208.

[43] The HUD study, entitled "Assessment of the Housing Market Impact of the Five Percent Tax Credit on New Home Purchases," was never published. It was prepared by the Division of Housing and Community Analysis within the Office of Policy Development and Research in HUD, at the request of Senator Brooke, and provided to him. The Federal Home Loan Bank Board analysis is reported in "FHLBB Says $2,000 Tax Credit Is Not Stimulating Enough Home Sales," *Housing and Development Reporter*, July 14, 1975, p. 193.

especially to favor homeownership, and a body of research investigating the impact of the tax laws on housing has grown up over the past two decades.

The most important provisions of the tax law are:

1. The deductibility from income of mortgage interest and property taxes, which usually represent much more than half of the annual expenses of homeownership
2. The exclusion from income of the imputed rental value of owner-occupied housing
3. The special treatment of capital gains received upon the sale of a home. The gain is not taxed at all if the seller buys another home of at least equal value within eighteen months, and ultimately escapes taxation entirely when the seller is over fifty-five. In 1978 Congress also permitted a one-time exclusion of up to $100,000 in capital gains, regardless of age or purchase of another home.

The first two categories are not unique to owner-occupied housing. Interest paid for almost any reason is deductible, as are most state and local taxes. The imputed income accruing to an owner-occupant does not differ conceptually from the services provided by any other consumer durable such as a car or home appliance; the law makes no attempt to tax the benefits received by ownership of any durable good, because no money or other consideration changes hands and it would be difficult to estimate the annual rental value of houses, refrigerators, etc., for millions of individual units. The capital gains treatment, however, is unusual, and is in addition to the exclusion of 60 percent of a long-term gain that now applies to all other assets.

Owners of rental housing receive only the first of these tax benefits. They are able to deduct interest and property taxes as business expenses, but they cannot exclude the rental income they receive from their other income for tax purposes. The capital gains treatment also differs. Landlords cannot roll over the capital gain by buying a new property, or escape taxation altogether by remaining in business until the age of fifty-five. On the other hand, landlords have some benefits not available to owners; they can claim accelerated depreciation on the property, as discussed in chapter 3, and can also deduct maintenance, utilities, and other operating costs as business expenses.

In the context of the present chapter, the tax treatment of homeowners and rental property is of interest to the extent that it affects the tenure choice decision; also of interest is the question of whether some alternative tax provisions would encourage homeownership to a greater extent. Unfortunately, the professional literature in economics and other disciplines on tenure choice largely ignores taxes and, in addition, fails to consider the importance in general of the relative cost of owning versus renting, which the tax laws are designed to affect. Instead, it relates the decision to own to the income of the household, its wealth, and its demographic characteristics (for example, the age of the head of the household, the number of children, and marital status). These are important factors, but they generally lie outside the scope of public policy.

Public discussion of the tax treatment of homeownership has generally centered on questions of equity and of the "tax expenditures" or revenue reductions incurred by the federal government as a result of the deductions and exclusions. The progressive nature of the federal income tax means that deductions reduce tax liability by a greater fraction of income for high-income households than for low-income ones, since the marginal tax bracket of the household rises with income. In addition, homeownership increases with income. For both reasons, the tax reduction per household from the interest and property tax deductions is higher for higher-income households. This is sometimes perceived to be "unfair," and there has been increasing interest among policy makers in finding some form of tax benefit to homeowners that would help middle- and lower-income families to a greater extent, while reducing the tax benefits of higher-income households whose tenure choice decision would probably be unaffected by the change.[44]

The first analysis of tax benefits to attract attention among policy makers was Henry Aaron's calculation of the savings to homeowners from the deductibility of mortgage interest and taxes and the exclusion of imputed rent.[45] Aaron estimated that these had resulted in a $7 billion tax saving in 1966. The bulk of this accrued to families with incomes above $15,000, and the savings were distributed regressively, reducing the tax liability of richer households by a greater share of income. However, a change in the tax laws which would include imputed income and eliminate the deduction for interest and taxes at the same time would discriminate against homeownership, as compared with renting, since the deductions for interest and taxes are available to landlords—and indeed to any other business person—

---

[44] See, for example, the statement of then presidential candidate Jimmy Carter in *Business Week*, May 3, 1976, p. 65.

[45] Henry Aaron, "Income Taxes and Housing," *American Economic Review*, vol. 60 (December 1970), pp. 789–806; see also Henry J. Aaron, *Shelter and Subsidies* (Washington, D.C.: Brookings Institution, 1972).

as business expenses. A more nearly neutral situation could be achieved by taxing the imputed rent of owner-occupied houses while continuing to allow the deductions. Tax revenues with this change would have risen by $4 billion, according to Aaron; again, most of the remaining $3 billion in tax savings would accrue to the well-to-do, in a regressive pattern, although the richest households (with incomes above $100,000) would benefit least as a percentage of income.

Aaron also estimated the tax revenues lost from accelerated depreciation on rental property. This would depend on the tax bracket of the landlord; for a 40 percent bracket and a true depreciation rate of 2 percent per year, the reduction would have been about $6.3 billion in 1966—not much smaller than the benefits to homeowners.

The tax benefits are quite large compared with the costs of other housing programs. The National Housing Policy Review, for example, estimated the cost of all of the subsidized programs for low-income families at $2.5 billion for calendar year 1972.[46]

Effect on Homeownership. Aaron explicitly did not attempt to analyze the impact of any change in the tax laws on either the tenure choice decision or the value of housing occupied by owners or renters, though acknowledging that "reactions to any large change in tax liability would be substantial."[47] The similarity of the estimates of tax benefits for owners and landlords suggests that, in a very gross way, the income tax laws were not exceptionally favorable to ownership, although Aaron did not consider all the differences in tax treatment, and the changes in the laws since 1966 have probably encouraged homeownership. Any serious estimate of the impact of taxes on tenure must look at the distribution across income classes of the net benefits from owning.

A more detailed and sophisticated analysis of the tax laws by Litzenberger and Sosin suggests that the current laws in fact encourage relatively low-income households to rent, middle- and upper-income households to own, and upper-income households to be landlords.[48] This occurs because of the progressive nature of the tax system and because of competition in the housing market. The tax savings available to landlords will, in a competitive market, be reflected in rents, so that low-income families will find that renting is more eco-

---

[46] National Housing Policy Review, *Housing in the Seventies*, p. 95.

[47] Aaron, "Income Taxes and Housing," p. 791, n. 6.

[48] Robert H. Litzenberger and Howard B. Sosin, "Taxation and the Incidence of Homeownership across Income Groups," paper presented at the meetings of the Allied Social Science Associations, Toronto, Canada, December 1977.

nomical than owning, since their own tax brackets are too low to yield much of a tax saving from ownership. This analysis represents a substantial advance on previous work and indicates that the relationship between taxes and tenure is quite complex. Litzenberger and Sosin do not, however, attempt to quantify their work or to estimate the income level at which ownership becomes preferable to renting.

The only recent effort to calculate the impact of taxes on tenure is that by Tolley and Diamond.[49] They work through the effect of the tax treatment of each component of housing expenses on the cost of owning in relation to the cost of renting in a newly constructed project, on the assumption that the marginal tax bracket of the landlord is 40 percent. They then compare this relative price to the incidence of homeownership, across income classes. They find that ownership increases to a much greater extent, for a given change in the relative price, for lower-income households. At incomes above $10,000 to $15,000, in 1969 dollars, tenure shows very little responsiveness to price changes. Their findings are consistent with the marked increase in homeownership that has occurred since 1970 concomitantly with the increase, resulting largely from inflation, in the marginal tax bracket of the typical household. The validity of the study, however, is limited by the fact that the tax treatment of rental housing is restricted to newly constructed projects. As has been noted in chapter 3, the tax benefits to existing rental property are smaller.

Tax Credits. Both of these recent studies suggest that homeownership among lower-income households could be increased if tax credits were substituted for the current system of deductions, without greatly lowering the extent of homeownership among higher-income households. A tax credit would be less regressive than a deduction, because the amount of the tax saving would be the same in all marginal tax brackets, and thus at all income levels. The tax credit has sometimes received public attention as an alternative to the present deductions, both for equity reasons and as a means of encouraging homeownership; for example, in 1979 the House Ways and Means Committee considered such a credit for first-time home buyers with incomes of up to $28,000 as a substitute for local mortgage revenue bonds.[50]

Litzenberger and Sosin conclude that a general credit (not limited to former renters or households in a particular income range) would

---

[49] George S. Tolley and Douglas B. Diamond, "Homeownership, Rental Housing, and Tax Incentives," in U.S. Congress, House, Committee on Banking, Finance, and Urban Affairs, *Federal Tax Policy and Urban Development*, 95th Cong., 1st sess., June 1977.
[50] "Ways and Means Votes Modest Income Single-Family Bonds on 3 Year Trial," *Housing Affairs Letter*, no. 79–29 (July 20, 1979), pp. 3–4.

increase homeownership for low-income families: the extent would depend on the down payment requirements. They also find that the tax benefits would be reduced for high-income households. However, the credit would probably still be somewhat regressive. Tolley and Diamond do not address this question specifically, but their calculations suggest that lower- and middle-income households would be inclined to switch to owning, since their tenure choice decision is especially sensitive to relative prices and the credit would lower the relative price of owning. Higher-income households, on the other hand, would probably not shift to renting to any marked extent, since they are less sensitive to relative prices.

While a shift to a tax credit might thus increase the overall incidence of homeownership, it could reduce the amount of housing purchased or rented by higher-income households and thus reduce the value of the housing stock and the importance of housing production in the American economy. None of the studies have attempted to quantify this phenomenon, however.

The available evidence suggests that a tax credit might increase homeownership among lower-income households, but there is still ample room for further research, particularly concerning the actual quantitative effects on homeownership. In our present state of knowledge, it seems likely that such a change would have a number of unexpected side effects. Moreover, the choice between credits and deductions is a fundamental one and involves far more than simply the differential impact on tenure choice—important as that may be. At present, any drastic change seems unlikely for the foreseeable future, which affords time for the additional analysis that is clearly needed.

8

The Cost of Producing Houses

All of the actual and proposed programs discussed in the previous chapter attempt to lower the price of buying a home to the *buyer* in some way. They do not affect the cost of building the houses; the real resources required to construct them remain unchanged. New home prices could, of course, be reduced if building costs were reduced, and this alternative method of making homeownership more widely affordable has attracted the attention of policy makers and analysts ever since rapidly rising prices have been regarded as a serious national issue. Technological progress in home building has often been viewed as a solution to the cost problem. Such progress certainly can, and does, occur without government action, but proposals to stimulate innovation through government action have been common. This chapter discusses the most commonly perceived problems affecting the cost of building homes and considers various possible federal actions that have been suggested as means of dealing with the problems.

Building Technology

The "conventional wisdom" has long been that the housing industry is technologically backward. The Joint Committee on Housing looked into the state of the industry in 1949 and reported:

> The investigations of the committee confirm the general belief that the house-building industry has lagged behind other industries in the extent of its industrial and technical development. This is an important contributing factor to the high cost of housing and the past inability of the industry to provide an adequate volume of new construction. A majority of the houses being produced today are built by the

same handicraft methods which were used 50 years ago.[1]

The committee recommended a program of technical housing research into ways to reduce housing costs.[2] Twenty years later the Kaiser Committee referred to a common view that "construction has lagged seriously behind most other segments of the economy in rate of productivity growth."[3] And ten years later still, the HUD Task Force on Housing Costs noted that "many proposals to cut housing costs over the last several decades have focused on American technological ingenuity."[4] This popular opinion underlay at least one federal demonstration program, Operation Breakthrough, in which over 25,000 homes were planned, using new construction methods and products. The program was designed, in particular, to encourage the use of industrialized—or mass—production rather than the traditional "handicraft system" of on-site building referred to by the joint committee in 1949. Over $72 million was spent in Operation Breakthrough between 1969 and 1974 in the hope that the new technology would prove both cost-effective and popular.

However, at the same time that this view was being generally accepted and propagated, several studies of the building industry were coming to the opposite conclusion. In an analysis prepared for the Kaiser Committee, Christopher Sims argued that there had been substantial technological progress in construction since World War II, with productivity per man-hour increasing about as rapidly as in the economy as a whole. This represented a change from the preceding two decades, when there had been "little or no efficiency growth."[5] The Kaiser Committee itself apparently found Sims's work persuasive enough to demur from the common view, concluding that "the industry is probably much more efficient and rationally organized than is popularly thought. . . . The housing industry is operating with at least modest efficiency and has experienced more technological advances than the casual observer would suspect." It is interesting, in the light of the Operation Breakthrough approach that was initiated a year later, to note that the Kaiser Committee found that "American housing producers, using rather conventional con-

---

[1] U.S. Congress, Joint Committee on Housing, *Housing Study and Investigation: Final Majority Report*, part 1, 80th Cong., 2nd sess., March 15, 1949, pp. 15–16.

[2] Ibid., pp. 1–2.

[3] U.S. President's Committee on Urban Housing (Kaiser Committee), *A Decent Home*, 1969, p. 121.

[4] U.S. Department of Housing and Urban Development, *Final Report of the Task Force on Housing Costs*, May 1978, p. 43.

[5] Christopher A. Sims, "Efficiency in the Construction Industry," in *Report of the President's Committee on Urban Housing: Technical Studies*, 1968, vol. 2, pp. 145–76. The quotation is from p. 156.

struction methods, have begun to compete in foreign markets, but
. . . foreign builders have yet to make a serious try to enter the U.S.
market."[6] Mass production is much more common in Europe than
in the United States.

Five years later the National Housing Policy Review (NHPR)
reported that technological progress was continuing; it noted that
many components of a house were assembled away from the site,
sometimes through the use of mass production techniques.[7] However, the process of technological change described by the NHPR and
later observers has been one of many relatively small improvements
gradually cumulating over a period of years, rather than being one
of large, dramatic "breakthroughs."[8]

Operation Breakthrough itself has probably not achieved its major objectives, although these objectives, like those of many government programs, were never stated in readily measurable terms. An
evaluation by the Urban Institute concluded that the project probably
did not stimulate significant technological innovation;[9] this opinion
was shared by most of the builders surveyed subsequently by the
U.S. General Accounting Office.[10] Nor did the project demonstrate
that the new technologies were less expensive than the traditional
building techniques. Ironically, the contributions of this massive effort to induce technological change have probably themselves been
small and incremental, causing some new firms to enter the industrialized housing industry and perhaps encouraging some minor
innovations.

The project thus appears to have demonstrated the opposite of
its original intention: Technological progress in housing continues to
be a process of gradual improvements, some of which may have been
expedited to a minor extent by Operation Breakthrough.[11]

---

[6] President's Committee on Urban Housing, *A Decent Home*, pp. 120–21.

[7] National Housing Policy Review, *Housing in the Seventies*, 1974, chap. 7.

[8] Nathaniel H. Rogg, "Comments," in Federal Home Loan Bank of San Francisco,
Resources for Housing (San Francisco: Federal Home Loan Bank of San Francisco, 1976),
pp. 195–204, especially p. 199; Department of Housing and Urban Development, *Task
Force on Housing Costs*, pp. 43–44.

[9] Donald R. Weidman, Francine L. Tolson, and Joseph S. Wholey, *Summary of Initial
Assessment and Evaluation Study Design for Operation Breakthrough* (Washington, D.C.:
The Urban Institute, 1974), p. 8.

[10] U.S. General Accounting Office, Comptroller General, *Operation Breakthrough: Lessons
Learned about Demonstrating New Technology*, November 2, 1976, pp. 23–24.

[11] Private assessments of Operation Breakthrough have generally been unfavorable.
See Rogg, "Comments," p. 199; and Martin Mayer, *The Builders* (New York: W.W.
Norton and Co., 1978), pp. 264–67 and 272–75.

Building Codes

One special concern has been that technological progress may be hampered by local building codes which unduly restrict the use of new materials and methods. This idea can be traced back to at least the end of World War II, when the Joint Committee on Housing blamed the codes in part for the backwardness of the construction industry, stating that they "have become an impediment to more efficient methods of home building and to the introduction of new materials and new construction techniques."[12] The committee recommended a federal effort to promote standardized building codes. This view remains popular; the 1978 HUD Task Force on Housing Costs estimated that perhaps 10,000 political jurisdictions have building codes and that "this uncoordinated system of differing and increasing regulation is slowing down the building process and making the adoption of current and new potential cost-saving ideas more difficult and expensive."[13]

There have been a number of studies of the effect of building codes on housing costs; although the impact is difficult to quantify, most if not all of these studies have found it to be small. Two studies conducted at the behest of the Kaiser Committee estimated the savings to lie in the range of 1.5 to 7.5 percent.[14] These studies were based on surveys of the codes of communities in different areas of the country, which compared their provisions to suggested standards recommended by the National Association of Home Builders. A review of the literature on the costs of codes prepared for the National Housing Policy Review estimated that building codes increased home costs by between 5 and 10 percent.[15]

Most recently, the General Accounting Office surveyed eighty-seven communities and found that the typical community's code raised the cost of a home by about $1,700 above what it would be if all of the materials and methods favored by builders were incorpo-

---

[12] Joint Committee on Housing, *Housing Study and Investigation*, p. 15.
[13] Department of Housing and Urban Development, *Task Force on Housing Costs*, p. 35.
[14] Ralph J. Johnson, "Housing Technology and Housing Costs," in *Report of the President's Committee on Urban Housing: Technical Studies*, vol. 2, pp. 53–64; and Leland S. Burns and Frank Mittelbach, "Efficiency in the Housing Industry," in the same work, vol. 2, pp. 75–144; see especially pp. 99–102. Johnson estimates the cost at 5.0 to 7.5 percent; Burns and Mittelbach estimate it at 1.5 to 3.0 percent. The latter study is much more detailed.
[15] George Sternlieb and David Listokin, "Building Codes: State of the Art, Strategies for the Future," report submitted to the National Housing Policy Review, June 1973.

rated in the codes.[16] This represented about 3.5 percent of the price of a typical new house at the time. GAO concluded that codes were not a major contributor to housing prices but that some savings were possible. It noted, however, that some of the less expensive items included in its surveys were not used by builders even where they were permitted, and it attributed this, in part at least, to consumer preferences for the more expensive materials.

There have been few serious academic studies of the effect of codes on housing costs. Muth and Wetzler estimated that savings might be around 2 percent if codes were less restrictive; this estimate was based on a multiple regression analysis of 1966–1967 average FHA new home prices, net of site value, across metropolitan areas.[17] This effect was not statistically significant, however.

As with building technology, federal housing policy has occasionally attempted to remedy the perceived problems created by building codes. Congress established the National Institute of Building Sciences (NIBS) in 1974, partly to evaluate new technology and to facilitate the adoption of that technology by localities. NIBS is supposed to serve as an authoritative national source of information in lieu of the seventy-five different associations and technical groups previously involved in testing and approving new methods and materials. Its creation had been recommended by the Douglas Commission in 1968.

A further step which has attracted some support is the establishment of a national building code, replacing the diverse local codes now in existence. Such a step would be highly controversial,[18] and policy makers are usually careful to avoid saying that they favor it. The Task Force on Housing Costs, for example, explicitly stated: "We do not recommend that Congress and the Administration act to preempt states and localities in the building codes area by federally requiring a national building code."[19] Nevertheless, federal policy on specific issues has tended to require increasing uniformity among localities, through standards for energy conservation and safety, for

---

[16] U.S. General Accounting Office, Comptroller General, *Why Are New House Prices So High, How Are They Influenced by Government Regulations, And Can Prices Be Reduced?* May 11, 1978, chap. 5.

[17] Richard F. Muth and Elliot Wetzler, "The Effect of Constraints on House Costs," *Journal of Urban Economics*, vol. 3 (January 1976), pp. 57–67.

[18] For a discussion of views on a national building code, see Rudard A. Jones, "A Rationale for Government Intervention in Housing: Diversity in Community Building Codes Acts to Constrain the National Effectiveness of the Housing Technical Community," in National Housing Policy Review, *Housing in the Seventies: Working Papers*, vol. 1, pp. 531–38.

[19] Department of Housing and Urban Development, *Task Force on Housing Costs*, p. 37.

example, and through the Minimum Property Standards for FHA homes. It seems likely that further federalization of local codes will occur.

For several reasons it is doubtful that any such federalization would lower housing costs. The conservation and safety standards are more likely to raise costs, in the name of higher national purposes. There is already a federal code for mobile homes which imposes higher standards than had previously been applied under the code advocated by the mobile home manufacturers and widely adopted; the higher standards have clearly raised the costs of mobile homes. It seems probable that any federal code for conventional homes would tend to have the same effect. The political incentives for a federal code agency would lie in the direction of greater safety and better housing, so as to minimize the risk of individual "horror stories" of unsafe or shoddy homes, however isolated such incidents might be. This pattern has been found in many federal regulatory agencies.

Moreover, with a single national code it would probably be more difficult than at present for new technology to be adopted. Decisions now are made locally, and a new product or technique can receive a market test if it is adopted in any of the 10,000 jurisdictions with building codes or by any builder operating in a location *without* a code. The new technology, then, has the opportunity to demonstrate its superiority (or inferiority) in the marketplace.

The expected process of changing a federal code can be inferred from the current practices followed in changing the model codes now in existence. At present there are four such model codes, each promulgated by a different national organization of building officials. The process of modifying these codes is complicated. Subcommittees of the groups first hear arguments on both sides from interested parties, who are usually the producers or trade associations directly affected. The subcommittees make recommendations to the parent organization, which then debates and passes on the change at an annual meeting. As might be expected, considerable pressure is often brought to bear by the interested groups, since the effect of the code group's decision on them may be substantial. One student of the code-change process concluded that, "More often than not the politics of national trade associations are played just as heavily at the model code meeting as at the city hall."[20] This political climate exists even though the model codes are not binding on the localities which adopt

---

[20] Francis T. Ventre, *Maintaining Technological Currency in the Local Building Code: Patterns of Communication and Influence*, Urban Data Service Reports, vol. 3, no. 4 (Washington, D.C.: International City Management Association, April 1971), p. 3.

them: the communities can and often do make whatever modifications they choose. With a single national code, to whatever extent it is binding on localities, there is only one entity which can approve the new technology. It is highly likely that "the politics of national trade associations" would be played still more fiercely at the offices of the federal agency responsible for the code.

Promulgation of a federal building code raises many issues beyond that of housing costs, such as preemption of local decision-making powers. From the standpoint of the effect on costs, it seems unlikely that such a code could or would lower costs in any significant way. Indeed, the research to date suggests that local codes at present have a minor impact on costs. It seems far more likely that costs would be *raised* rather than lowered, as the rate of introduction of new technology—and its diffusion—would be slowed.

Land and Development Costs

While the "problems" of building codes and technological progress have been discussed for many years, another input into the production of new homes has only recently attracted attention as a cause of the rise in prices. Land has apparently been constituting a growing share of the cost of the home, and builders have become increasingly concerned about land and development costs. The rise in the price of "raw" land, while greater than the increases in costs of other inputs, has been viewed by builders and policy makers as somewhat less of a problem than the costs imposed by local governments in their regulation of land use and development. A recent study by Stephen Seidel concluded that regulations affecting the price of land, such as zoning and environmental constraints, composed the second largest number of regulations confronting the builder, while subdivision approval regulations (concerning streets, sewers, and water lines, for example) composed the largest group. Builders felt that both categories contributed far more to "unnecessary" cost increases than did building codes or financial regulations.[21]

Zoning. By far the oldest form of land use regulation is zoning. Zoning can affect both the use to which land may be put and the size of a given land parcel devoted to any use. The latter type of zoning ordinance creates much greater concern among builders, because,

---

[21] Stephen R. Seidel, *Housing Costs and Government Regulation: Confronting the Regulatory Maze* (New Brunswick, N.J.: Rutgers University, Center for Urban Policy Research, 1978), pp. 19, 37–38.

150

typically, single-family homes may be built on land zoned for any "lower" purpose, such as for apartments or for commercial or industrial use. Since these lot-size requirements are established locally, they can and do vary substantially across the country. The GAO survey of eighty-seven communities found minimum lot sizes varying from 4,500 feet to two acres; the largest was thus nineteen times the smallest. However, only about 10 percent had minimums larger than a half acre, and the typical minimum was about a quarter acre.[22] Seidel found a similar pattern, but with a smaller typical minimum—around one-fifth of an acre.[23]

The effect of these requirements on housing costs is not clear. Undoubtedly a high minimum lot size raises the ultimate cost of a house if one is actually built on the lot; but it also creates an inducement for builders and buyers to look elsewhere. Unless large lot sizes are uniform in a metropolitan area or housing market, their impact is likely to be greater in diverting the pattern of development than in raising housing costs directly, although they may still have some effect on costs. Moreover, minimum lot sizes appear to be positively related to the income level of the people already living in the community. This may represent a kind of "fiscal zoning" or a community consensus to keep lower-income families out of high-income areas. It also suggests that families seeking to buy their first house, who are likely to have relatively low incomes, are not being directly priced out of the new home market by lot size requirements—unless they are unwilling to live in areas occupied largely by people with similar incomes.[24]

Systematic studies of the impact of lot-size zoning on land costs are rare, in contrast to a larger literature on the effect of land use constraints. It is relatively easy to show that sales price is related to lot size, but this does not document the effect of the zoning, since it is possible that the regulation may reflect the expected preference of buyers.[25] Some studies have concluded that the latter is frequently

---

[22] Comptroller General, *Why Are New House Prices So High?*, p. 20.

[23] Seidel, *Housing Costs and Government Regulations*, p. 174.

[24] Ibid., p. 177.

[25] An example of this type of study is Lynne B. Sagalyn and George Sternlieb, *Zoning and Housing Costs* (New Brunswick, N.J.: Rutgers University, Center for Urban Policy Research, 1973), chap. 3; see especially pp. 54–55 and 66–69. Their regression results show that sales prices could be reduced by about 3.2 percent with a 25 percent reduction in lot size, and another 1.5 percent with a 12 percent reduction in lot frontage. (These calculations are derived from exhibit III–8, p. 63, and information on p. 68.) Whether these numbers are large or small is a matter for individual opinion; but the study does not demonstrate that the lot size and frontage result from zoning constraints, so there is no way of knowing whether any such reduction would actually occur.

the case; an analysis of the Boston metropolitan area found that zoning had little effect on lot sizes because the minimums were generally set just above the size that would be established in the market were there no zoning.[26]

Environmental Constraints. New forms of land use regulation have arisen out of public concern over the environment. These regulations have, typically, been developed at the state level; ten states now have some form of land use control, at least in part for environmental purposes. Usually, builders are required to submit environmental impact statements broadly similar to those now required for major federal projects and programs. The requirements for an environmental impact statement vary from state to state in terms of the size of development for which statements must be prepared, the information that must be provided, and the review process. These requirements can impose three different costs on builders and buyers: the actual expense of preparing the statement, the cost of delay while the statement is being prepared and (particularly) approved, and the costs of changes required by the government before approval is granted.

There have been a few studies of the costs of these environmental constraints. An analysis of Florida and California requirements by Muller and James found that these costs were small, amounting to 0.4 percent of the new home price in San Diego County and 0.7 percent in Broward County (Fort Lauderdale). The costs of delay accounted for most of this in both cases.[27] This study suggests that, so far at least, these constraints have not imposed significant cost increases on new home buyers.

Additional environmental constraints are sometimes imposed in the coastal areas of various states in response to the federal Coastal Zone Management Act, passed in 1972. Several states have established agencies with review powers over developments in coastal areas in the interests of preserving their amenities. Again, the cost of these constraints undoubtedly varies from state to state, although little has been done to study them. An analysis of the review process in one New Jersey township found that costs generated by the coastal zone regulations were about $135 for a house and $125 for an apartment—much less than 1 percent of total land acquisition and devel-

[26] *Urban Land Value As It Relates to Policy* (Lexington, Mass.: Urban Land Research Analysts Corporation, December 1969), pp. 117–21. No authors are listed on the title page of this publication, but the summary identifies Larry D. Orr and William P. Travis as principal researchers.

[27] Franklin J. James and Thomas Muller, "Environmental Impact Evaluation, Land Use Planning, and the Housing Consumer," *AREUEA Journal*, vol. 5 (Fall 1977), pp. 279–301.

opment costs. Total regulatory costs were estimated at about one-third and one-fourth of overall land costs.[28]

At the same time, it seems clear that the direct effects of raising costs on those homes actually built is less important than the indirect effect of diverting development to noncoastal areas. Studies of both New Jersey and California found that the share of building in coastal areas declined after the state laws were put into effect, and in California, at least, prices of existing homes in the coastal zone went up much more rapidly than inland.[29] Whatever its effect on new home prices, the coastal zone regulations have enhanced the wealth of those already living there at the expense of those not so fortunate. The regulations may also be making it disproportionately more difficult for lower-income families to move into the coastal area. Muller and James estimated that the impact would be concentrated among the lowest-priced units as builders sought to protect the value of their investments in the land by building the most expensive houses for which they could find a market.[30]

Subdivision requirements and related land development restrictions are regarded as still more onerous by builders. They include regulations on street width and thickness of pavement, similar regulations for sidewalks (including the requirement that there be any at all) and driveways, specifications of size and materials for water main and storm sewer pipes, curb and gutter requirements for drainage, requirements for manhole spacing, and land dedication or in-lieu fees for local parks and schools.

These regulations are locally imposed and, as with the zoning and environmental restrictions, it is difficult to get an overall picture of their national impact. The GAO study cited earlier listed seventeen subdivision requirements and surveyed its eighty-seven communities to determine how many imposed higher standards than those recommended by builders. It then estimated the cost of each higher standard. Not surprisingly, the communities varied markedly; the effect on costs ranged from $2,655 per house down to zero in two communities which accepted all of the builders' recommendations. The median was about $1,300 per house, or about 2.5 percent of the

---

[28] Dan K. Richardson, *The Cost of Environmental Protection* (New Brunswick, N.J.: Rutgers University, Center for Urban Policy Research, 1976), chap. 7.

[29] The New Jersey data are taken from Seidel, *Housing Costs and Government Regulations,* p. 255; the California data are from Michael R. Peevey, "The Coastal Plan and Jobs: A Critique," *The California Coastal Plan: A Critique* (San Francisco, Calif.: Institute for Contemporary Studies, 1976), pp. 93–105.

[30] James and Muller, "Environmental Impact Evaluation," pp. 298–99.

price of the typical new home being built at the time.[31] This is less than the study's estimate of the cost of building code requirements.

Other quantitative information on the effect of subdivision requirements is scanty. Some indirect evidence can be obtained from analysis of the Census Bureau's new home price index, however. Before 1974 this index did not adjust the home price for the size of the lot; since 1974 it has done so, and has published indices both with and without lot size held constant. Surprisingly, prices have risen faster for the latter index.[32] If land and development costs were increasing in importance, builders and buyers should be reacting by reducing the lot size as much as possible (given the zoning constraints on minimum lot size); the smaller lots would tend to hold down the price increase in the index in which they were not taken into account. Instead, the opposite pattern occurs. This comparison is not as precise as is desirable, since there are other differences between the two indices. A special index was constructed by the Census Bureau for HUD, which compares price changes with and without lot size held constant (with no other differences between the indices) for 1974 and 1975; the two indices showed identical changes nationally over the two years.[33]

Thus, it does not appear that any of the land use and development restrictions discussed have had a significant impact on housing prices, at least on a national basis. This, however, should not be construed as minimizing their effect. Cumulatively, these restrictions may well have a measurable effect on house prices, particularly in those areas where many types of restrictions are especially severe. And some of the restrictions are too new for their impact to be evaluated with any degree of confidence. But the evidence available so far does not indicate that they have had a substantial effect.

Given this evidence, why is there so much concern among builders and policy makers? The reason appears to be that the standards are local: they may impose substantial costs on some builders and buyers in some areas. These are the builders who complain most loudly; those who do not confront the problems have no reason to make an issue of their *lack* of problems. In a series of hearings on housing costs around the country, a task force of the House Subcommittee on Housing and Community Development found a mixed pattern; builders in some areas were greatly concerned about land

---

[31] Comptroller General, *Why Are New House Prices So High?*, pp. 14–19.

[32] U.S. Bureau of the Census, *Price Index of New One-Family Homes Sold*, Fourth Quarter 1977, series C27–77–Q4, tables 1 and 4.

[33] U.S. President, *Ninth Annual Report on the National Housing Goal*, 95th Cong., 1st sess., January 1977, pp. 92–97; see especially table C–16.

use and development regulations, while builders in other areas did not even mention them.[34] And there is no national organization that systematically collects information on the local regulations, so that little is known even about the pattern of regulation, let alone about its economic impact. Also, it is possible for builders to shift their operations to locations that have less restrictive ordinances, even within metropolitan areas. This apparently is occurring. Land use and development regulations are incorporated in the building permit issuance process; areas that do not issue permits have, perforce, no regulations. In recent years an increasing share of new home building has been occurring outside of permit-issuing jurisdictions.

The role of federal policy in mitigating the effects of these local regulations is indirect and, so far at least, tentative. The recent HUD Task Force on Housing Costs gave special attention to land and development costs as a major factor in new home price increases.[35] It recommended a HUD program of technical information to local and state governments in devising land use and development standards (somewhat like the role of NIBS in building technology). It also went further and recommended that regional land use and development standards be encouraged, with HUD monitoring local compliance with the regional standards and, if necessary, enforcing compliance by withholding federal urban development grants and other federal grants to states and localities.[36] This recommendation aroused intense political opposition when it was leaked before the release of the report, and HUD Secretary Patricia Harris explicitly disavowed it, indicating that she had no intention of recommending any such steps as federal policy.[37]

As with building codes, it is doubtful whether any federal standards would in fact be less restrictive than those of the localities, particularly given the evidence that the existing land use and development regulations have little effect on housing prices. The builders' recurrent complaints about FHA processing and red tape do not offer encouragement for the notion that a federal land use regulatory agency would be especially responsive to their concerns. Instead, intense political confrontations between developers and environ-

---

[34] U.S. Congress, House, Committee on Banking, Finance, and Urban Affairs, Subcommittee on Housing and Community Development, *Task Force on Homeownership*, 95th Cong., 2nd sess., 1978. The concern with environmental restrictions expressed by witnesses in Los Angeles contrasts markedly with the opinions of witnesses in Houston, for example.

[35] Department of Housing and Urban Development, *Task Force on Housing Costs*, p. 13.

[36] Ibid., pp. 15–16.

[37] Susanna McBee, "Harris Rejects Suggested Zoning, Land Use Guides," *Washington Post*, June 8, 1978, p. D20.

mentalists would probably occur continually, with numerous requests for local modifications of federal guidelines working their way through whatever decision-making and appeal process would be devised. It is hard to believe that such a process would *reduce* delays and expedite land development and house construction. The opposite is much more likely to occur.

9

Conclusion

To judge by what is commonly written about American housing, we have made little progress toward achieving our goals. Year after year we read over again that much of our housing is poor and that most of us cannot afford to buy homes. A 1976 *New York Times* editorial stated that "the nation has lived for so long with the sad reality of big city slums and of tar-paper shacks and tumbledown houses in half-hidden rural villages that a housing 'crisis' has come to be regarded as a permanent feature of the social landscape."[1] In a similar way, calculations showing how difficult it is to buy a new home go back at least 40 years to the report of the Temporary National Economic Committee, which said that only 24 percent of American families—those with incomes of at least $2,000—could afford the typical new home, then priced over $4,000. These figures look somewhat familiar; as Leo Grebler has observed, "Multiply by ten or twelve and you come close to current statistics of this type."[2] Truly, we appear to be on a treadmill.

But while the rhetoric is the same, the reality of housing has changed. When the Temporary National Economic Committee made its calculations, less than half of the population owned their own homes and the percentage was dropping. Today the figure is almost two-thirds, and rising. Three times as many families are homeowners today as in 1940. There has been a similar improvement in housing quality. The *New York Times* editorial referred to 5 million dwellings without adequate indoor plumbing, "families with small children

---

[1] "The Housing Issue," *New York Times*, October 21, 1976, p. 38.
[2] Leo Grebler, "Comments—The Cost of Housing: An Analysis of Trends, Incidence, and Causes," in Federal Home Loan Bank of San Francisco, *The Cost of Housing* (San Francisco: Federal Home Loan Bank of San Francisco, 1978), p. 43.

crowded into 'mobile homes,' " and "urban families that occupy one or two rooms in badly converted buildings originally erected as single-family residences."[3] The 5 million dwellings without adequate plumbing probably referred to 1970; the census that year reported 4.4 million units without plumbing, down from 7.6 million in 1960. By 1977 the figure for such units was 2.5 million—only 1.8 million of them occupied. Even 5 million would be a vast improvement over the recent past. About 1.4 million mobile homes (out of 3.7 million) were occupied by families with children, and about half of those had only one child. And while statistics are not kept on one- and two-room units in "badly converted single-family residences," there were only 3.0 million occupied one- and two-room dwellings altogether throughout the country in 1977, down from 3.1 million in 1970, and only half were located in central cities. Each of these figures represents less than 3 percent of the total housing stock. An editorial in 1950 could have complained about 15 million dwellings without complete plumbing and 4.5 million with only one or two rooms.

In a sense, the *New York Times* editorial had things backward; the nation has lived for a long time with the sad rhetoric of big city slums and tar-paper shacks, while in reality our housing has steadily improved.

Our housing quality is unique in the world. A Swiss official who had studied urban problems in the United States brought this home forcefully to the author at a European housing conference. "Tell me," he asked, "is there anyone here who can give you any useful advice about your housing problems—or even comprehend them? None of us could believe that people would actually *abandon* perfectly good housing in the middle of cities and go and live somewhere else." Abandonment is a complex phenomenon, partly related to government programs (such as Section 235 or rent control) but resulting also from other factors; it would not happen, however, were there not equally satisfactory housing available elsewhere.[4]

Unfortunately, housing policy has often been based on the rhetoric rather than the reality. We continue to provide help to the poor by building new apartments for them, at great expense, even though most of them already live in adequate housing or housing that can

---

[3] "The Housing Issue," p. 38.

[4] Strictly speaking, the statement in the text refers to abandonment by owner-occupants or vacating of premises by tenants. Landlords of rental property may abandon title to it, even though it is occupied, because they can no longer earn enough on the property to cover the out-of-pocket costs of running it. Should this happen, tenants could be forced to vacate even though they have not found equally satisfactory housing elsewhere. However, it is unlikely that landlords would be unable to earn anything on their property unless it is worse than most, if not all, other housing in the local market.

easily and cheaply be brought up to standard. And we have so far found that many of our efforts to devise programs to help people buy homes end up by subsidizing those who would probably have bought in any case, or else are successful at a high price—in scandal and corruption as well as money.

Undoubtedly, one major reason for the continued emphasis on building housing for the poor, and for the concern with the affordability of new homes, is macroeconomic—the desire to have a healthy housing construction industry as part of a healthy economy. This justification has been offered for each new program in turn. Few programs, if any, however, have made any discernible contribution to stability in housing construction, and there is little evidence that most of the housing actually built would not have been built in any case, without subsidy. Many of the programs are redistributive: they build housing for the poor which would otherwise probably be built for middle-income and upper-income families. But they are not very efficient mechanisms for changing the distribution of income.

There are real housing problems remaining, as well as real improvements. A diminishing number of Americans still live in substandard housing by our traditional definition, and many more live in housing that we are now beginning to define explicitly as inadequate, given our rising income and improved housing technology. The inflation of the past decade has increased both the difficulty and the importance of homeownership; those who rent lose out on the inflation-induced capital gains which owners have experienced. Most of the programs which we have, however, offer assistance that is incommensurate with the problems. Experience with the existing housing part of Section 8, and with the housing allowance, indicates that we can achieve the modest degree of improvement needed to bring many of our dwellings up to current quality standards and can provide significant financial relief for many hard-pressed poor families. New mortgage instruments are being devised and offered in the marketplace which are particularly attractive to younger families seeking to buy their first home, and which are winning acceptance at little or no cost to the federal government. These programs and instruments point the way to fruitful federal policies for the future.

In reality, we can surely expect further housing improvements between now and the end of the century, just as we have experienced them since the end of World War II. Most of the impetus for these improvements will come from rising incomes rather than from government programs. Whether our political rhetoric will catch up with the reality, and will create a climate of opinion conducive to programs directed at our real housing problems, remains to be seen.

APPENDIX

Definitions of
"Measures of Housing Inadequacy"

1. Lacking complete plumbing facilities (tub or shower, toilet, hot and cold piped water)
2. Crowded (more than 1.0 persons per room)
3. Lacking complete kitchen facilities (installed sink with piped water, range or cookstove, mechanical refrigerator)
4. One or more bedrooms lacking privacy (necessary to pass through bedroom to reach another bedroom or bathroom)
5. Three or more persons sharing a bedroom
6. Signs of mice or rats
7. Loose, broken, or missing steps on common stairways (for units located in apartment buildings)
8. Loose, broken, or missing stair railings on common stairways (for units located in apartment buildings)
9. Light fixtures in public halls not in working order (for units located in apartment buildings)
10. Exposed electrical wiring (not in walls or metal coverings)
11. One or more rooms lacking at least one electric wall outlet
12. Leaky basement
13. Leaky roof
14. Holes in the interior floor of the unit
15. Open cracks or holes in interior ceilings or walls
16. Broken plaster or peeling paint covering at least one square foot of ceiling or wall
17. Breakdown in water supply during previous three months
18. Lacking piped water
19. Breakdown in sewage disposal system during previous three months
20. Breakdown in toilet during previous three months (only for units with one toilet)
21. Electrical fuse blowout during previous three months
22. Breakdown in heating system during previous winter
23. Additional heat source (*had* to use additional sources of heat dur-

ing previous winter because regular heating system did not provide enough)

24. One or more rooms closed during previous winter because they could not be kept warm
25. One or more rooms with no heat during previous winter
26. Subfamily sharing unit (married couple with or without children, or one parent with one or more single children under 18 years living in household and related to head of household—e.g., young married couple sharing home or husband's or wife's parents)

SOURCE: U.S. Department of Housing and Urban Development and U.S. Bureau of the Census, *Annual Housing Survey: 1974, United States and Regions*, part B, appendix A.